NVIVO 9 ESSENTIALS

Your Guide to the World's Most Powerful Qualitative Data Analysis Software

By Bengt M. Edhlund

FORM & KUNSKAP AB
INFORMATIONTECHNOLOGY

FORM & KUNSKAP AB • P.O.BOX 4 • SE-645 06 STALLARHOLMEN • SWEDEN • +46 152 201 80
SALES@FORMKUNSKAP.COM • WWW.FORMKUNSKAP.COM

ISBN 978-1-4467-0762-3

NVIVO 9

NVivo 7 was launched in early 2006 and represented a comprehensive revision of NUD*IST and NVivo, two well known qualitative data analysis brands. QSR International Pte Ltd., which develops and markets NVivo, maintained a close collaboration with Microsoft. Since this collaboration began, Microsoft's current rules for graphical representation, user logic and language have had a great impact on NVivo's development policies and user procedures that are reflected in the NVivo since then.

Two years later QSR launched NVivo 8 to meet increasing demand for functionality and content stability. In addition to regular text documents, NVivo could now manage audio, video and pictures.

Now there is NVivo 9 which continued to evolve and provides advanced tools for text analysis and teamwork as well as a number of tools for graphical presentation of ongoing and completed research projects. NVivo 9 Server is a separate product module which allows users to work in a local network where team members can work simultaneously on the same material. Server module will be described in separate documentation. Everything described in this book applies the user procedures valid also for team collaboration with NVivo 9 Server.

TABLE OF CONTENTS

1. INTRODUCTION

This book is targeted to all those who work with qualitative research data. This book is for anyone involved in qualitative studies who has begun to realize that handling and organizing documents, copies, and multimedia data becomes unmanageable. NVivo helps researchers organize information for easy retrieval and analysis.

Perhaps many still remember the manual methods used in earlier times. Photocopying to a large extent, selecting text sections, markings and cuttings were commonplace. Certain texts may then have been lost in binders or paper piles somewhere. Using smart software like NVivo makes it possible to collect data with common topics in nodes that contain pointers to various sections of several documents.

Whether you apply grounded theory or you are working on phenomenology, ethnography, discourse analysis, attitude surveys, organizational studies or a combination of different methods you will soon realize the power of bringing order and structure to your data. It becomes easier and more efficient to verify theories and produce a better basis for discussion within a team. With NVivo data can usefully take the form of models or flow charts, or graphical representation of ideas and relationships.

Below is a simplified diagram of an NVivo project:

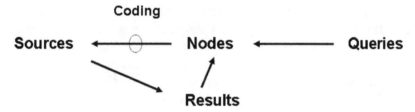

Source documents, nodes, and coding are the building blocks of your project. You will learn in-depth explanations of these concepts both in the logical journey through the chapters but also in the glossary that appears at the end of the book.

An NVivo project is the work material used in connection with a specific research assignments and who in some way be treated in terms of software NVivo. The project consists of one and only one project file that includes the digitalized material and pointers or links to external sources.

Within a project, NVivo conceptualizes data organization in terms of project items and folders. Items and folders in NVivo can be said to be virtual in relation to Windows environment. In an NVivo Project folders are similar to Windows folders, but NVivo has set up some rules for how they are handled (for example only certain types of folders are allowed to be organized hierarchically). Project Items correspond to files in the Windows environment and are handled in most cases like them. They may be edited, copied, cut, pasted, deleted, moved, etc., but they are all embedded a the project file.

Sources are documents, audio, video and image files, memos and other external items. When sources are imported or linked to NVivo they are mirrored as NVivo project items. Items like documents can also be created directly in NVivo's own word processor.

Memos are also items in a project. A memo is linked to a particular document or node. They can also be imported, but often they are created in NVivo.

Links of various kinds are important elements in an NVivo project. Links can be created between objects and to external sources.

A unique feature of NVivo is that certain types of items can be arranged hierarchically, namely nodes. Nodes are terms and concepts that are created during the process to designate properties, phenomena, or keywords that characterize sources or individual parts of the sources. Nodes are of different types: parent nodes, child nodes, relationships, and matrices.

Coding is the activity which means that words, sentences, whole paragraphs, other graphic elements or the whole object is associated with some nodes. Coding can take place only by items that are included in the project. An external source can not be encoded but the text is in the external object can be encoded.

Queries can recognize which parts of the project's sources that contain the desired information. A simple query is simply opening a node. Exploring more complex issues can involve combinations of nodes that are linked with Boolean operators. Queries can be saved to be reused as the projects develop. Results of queries can also be saved or be used to generate new nodes. Queries may also be in matrix form so that the rows of some nodes and columns of other nodes create a table where each cell is the result of two nodes and a particular operator.

An overall picture of how a project can be developed is:

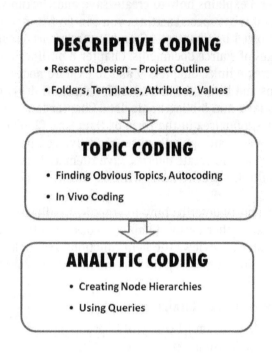

NVivo helps to organize data so that analysis and conclusions will be safer and easier. The ultimate goal may be described as follows:

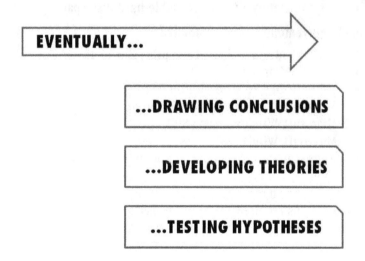

- ♦ -

The book is structured so that we start with the system requirements for software, then we describe in Chapter 2, how the screen is designed and the basic settings you can do for the software itself. Chapter 3 explains how to create, save and backup your project file and what special settings you can do for each project.

This is followed by Chapters 4-7 on how to import, create and edit different types of source documents. Chapter 8 outlines how to do memos and create links. Chapters 9 and 10 explore nodes, classifications and how they are created. Chapter 11 deals with literature reviews and bibliographic data. Chapter 12 moves into managing questionnairea in the form of Data Sets. Chapter 13 explains and goes systematically through NVivo coding, and Chapter 14-15 discusses how to create queries, save them and create nodes from the results. Chapter 16 deals with important aspects of working in teams.

Chapter 18 and 19 describe how to graphically illustrate a project using Models and other means, Chapter 20 describes the reporting methods, Chapter 21 reviews the help functions available, and Chapter 22 contains a glossary that occurs in connection with NVivo.

System Requirements – Minimum

- 1,2 GHz Pentium III-compatible processor or faster (32-bit); 1,4 GHz Pentium 4-processor (64-bit)
- 1 GB RAM
- 1024 x 768 screen resolution or higher
- Microsoft Windows XP SP2
- Approximately 1 GB of available hard-disk space

System Requirements – Recommended

- 2 GHz Pentium 4-compatible processor or faster
- 2 GB RAM or more
- 1280 x 1024 screen resolution or higher
- Microsoft Windows XP SP 2 or later; Microsoft Windows Vista SP 1; Microsoft Windows 7
- Approximately 2 GB of available hard-disk space
- Internet Connection

We recommend that your machine complies with those recommendations required for larger projects with over 5,000 documents even if you are working with smaller projects.

2. SCREEN ARCHITECTURE

This chapter is about the architecture of the NVivo screen which has a certain resemblance with Microsoft Outlook.

Appendix A, The NVivo Screen, (page 259), shows an overview of the NVivo window. We will use area **(1)**, area **(2)** etcetera to represent the various sectors of the NVivo window. A work session usually starts in area **(1)** with the selection of a Navigation Button corresponding to a group of folders. In area **(2)**, you select a certain folder, and area **(3)** the selection of a certain project item will lead to area **(4)** where you can study an open item.

Project work is done through the Ribbon menus, keyboard commands or or via the menu options broght up by right-clicking your mouse. Appendix C, (page 263), is a summary NVivo's keyboard commands and Appendix D, (page 267) is about the graphical conventions and typographical rules that have been used in this book.

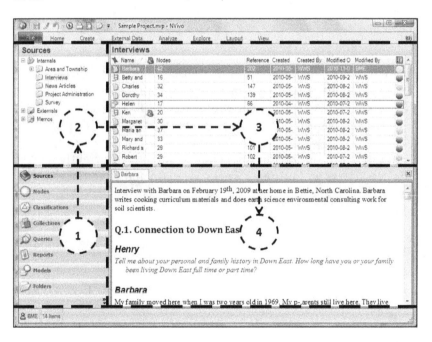

Below these four areas you will find the Status Bar that displays information (depending on the cursor position) on number of items in the current folder, number of nodes and references of the current item, and row number and column number of the current cursor position.

Area (1) - The Navigation Window

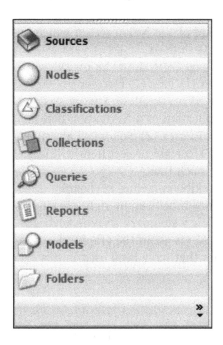

There are totally 8 navigation buttons. Down to the right is the >>-symbol with options on how to hide certain buttons and how to change the display order. Each button will display certain preselected folders in area (2) and the button [**Folders**] displays all folders.

In case a certain button that you need should be currently hidden you can always go to **Home** | **Workspace** | **Go** and from there to any navigation option. This menu also shows the corresponding key commands.

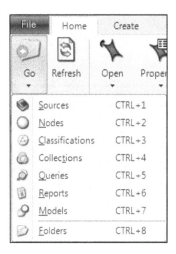

Area (2) – The Virtual Explorer

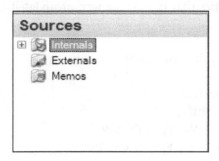

The folders associated with a Navigation Button are displayed here. The folders are virtual in relation to a Windows folder since they are stored in the project file. NVivo's folders perform like any Windows folder. Certain folders are predefined in the NVivo project template and cannot be changed or deleted whereas other folders can be created by the user. See page 46 on how to create and how to delete user defined folders.

The virtual file paths are called Hierarchical Names and are written with double backslash between virtual folders and single backslash between Parent Nodes and Child Nodes.

For example **Nodes\\Geographic\\County \ Beaufort**

Area (3) – The List View

Internals							
Name	Nodes	References	Created On	Created By	Modified On	Modified By	
Giorgi	0	0	2010-10-25 09:38	BME	2010-10-25 10:10	BME	
TwoColumns	3	6	2010-10-25 09:56	BME	2010-10-25 10:10	BME	
Peter	3	10	2010-10-25 10:10	BME	2010-10-25 10:26	BME	

Area (3) appears similar to a list of files in Windows, but NVivo terms these as Project Items within an Item List. All Project Items in the the folders Internals, Externals and Memos and their subfolders are source items. Folders are also items. The symbols for the various project items are found in Appendix B, page 261.

During the course of a project work you will need to revise the item lists when new items are being created, items are deleted and items are moved. At times it will be necessary to refresh the item list so that desired sorting is maintained.

♦ **Follow These Steps**
   1   Go to **Home | Workspace | Refresh**
      or key command [**F5**].

Properties

All items have certain characteristics that can be changed or updated whenever needed.

♦ **Follow These Steps**

1   Select the item in area **(3)** that you want to change or update.

2   Go to **Home | Item | Properties**
    or key command **[Ctrl] + [Shift] + [P]**
    or right-click and select **<Item type> Properties**.

The **Audio Properties** dialog box may appear like this:

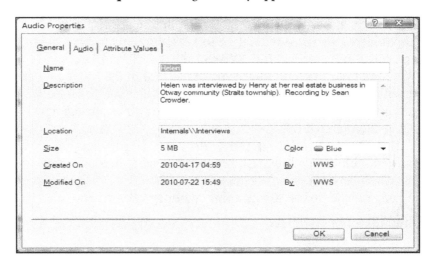

All information in this dialog box is editable and the text in the text boxes **Name** and **Description** is also searchable, see Chapter 14, Finding Project Items.

Color Mark an Item

Source items, nodes, relationships, attribute values or users can be color marked individually. NVivo has seven pre-defined colors. The color marking is shown in the List View of area **(3)** and can also be shown in Models and other visualizations and when using coding stripes.

♦ **Follow These Steps**

1   Select the item or items that you want to color mark.

2   Go to **Home | Item | Properties → Color → <select>**
    or right-click and select **Color → <select >**

Classifying an Item

All source items or nodes can be classified (see Chapter 10, About Classifications).

♦ **Follow These Steps**

1   Select the item or items that you want to classify.

2   Go to **Home | Item | Properties** → **Classification** →
    <select>
    or right-click and select **Classification** → **<select>**

List View Options

Default view option is the list as shown above. There other options
are: Small, Medium and Large Thumbnails.

♦   **Follow These Steps**
    1   Click on any empty space in area **(3)**.
    2   Go to **View | List View | List View** → **<select>**
    The result of choosing *Large Thumbnails* may appear like this:

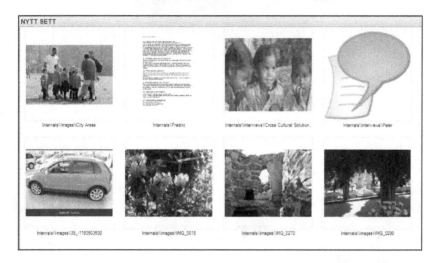

Display a Frame of a Video Item

Thumbnails of video items can display the specific frame that you
want.

♦   **Follow These Steps**
    1   Move the playhead the frame you want to display.
    2   Go to **Media | Selection | Assign Frame as Thumbnail**.
    The selected frame is displayed as a thumbnail in area **(3)** and
when using the Video tab för a node that the video item is coded at.

Sorting Options for a List

There are several ways to sort a list in area **(3)**.

♦   **Follow These Steps**
    1   Click on any empty space in area **(3)**.
    2   Go to **Layout | Sort & Filter | Sort by** → **<select>**
    You can also perform a custom sort by moving items in the list.

♦   **Follow These Steps**
    1   Select one or more items in area **(3)**.
    2   Go to **Layout | Rows & Columns | Move Up** ([Ctrl] + [Shift] + [U]).
    alternatively

2   Go to **Layout | Rows & Columns | Move Down** ([**Ctrl**] + [**Shift**] + [**D**]).

The sorting made like this is instantly stored as Custom Sorting and can at any later stage be resumed by going to **Layout | Sort & Filter | Sort by → Custom**.

Customize Current View of the Item List

♦   **Follow These Steps**

1   Click on any empty space in area (**3**).

2   Go to **View | List View | List View → Customize...**

The **Customize Current View** dialog box now appears:

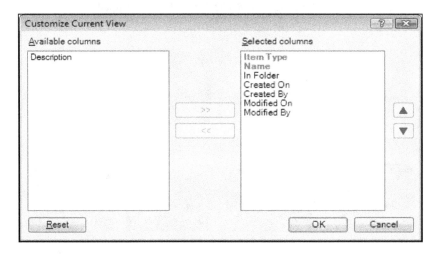

Printing the Item List

Printing the Item List is a valuable option during discussions in the project team.

♦   **Follow These Steps**

1   Go to **File → Print → Print List...**
    or right-click and select **Print → Print List...**

2   Select printer and printer settings, then [**OK**].

Exporting the Item List

It is possible to export the item list as a text file, a RTF file, an Excel spreadsheet or a Word document.

♦   **Follow These Steps**

1   Go to **External Data | Export | Export → Export List...**
    or right-click and select **Export → Export List...**

2   Select file format, folder and name, then [**OK**].

Area (4) – The Detail View

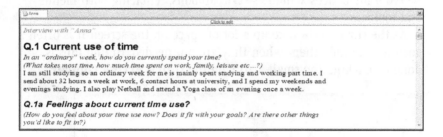

This is an example of an open Project Item, which could include a document, an audio, a video, a picture item, a memo, or a node. Each time a source item is opened it is Read Only. The document is made instantly editable by clicking on the *Click to edit* link at the top of an open item. Each item has its own tab when several items are opened at the same time.

Project Items are docked inside the main NVivo window. There is a possibility to undock these windows and maximize them as a separate window. An undocked item that is minimized is resumed with its program button on the Windows taskbar.

♦ **Follow These Steps**
   1   Go to **View | Workspace | Undock All**.

All open items will be undocked. Then any selected item can be docked again:

♦ **Follow These Steps**
   1   Select the undocked item.
   2   Go to **View | Workspace | Docked**.

or if you want to dock all open items:

♦ **Follow These Steps**
   1   Click outside any of the undocked items.
   2   Go to **View | Workspace | Dock All**.

The undocking of windows is only valid during an open work session; when you reopen a project all undocked windows are closed. However, you can go to **File → Options** and in the **Application Options** dialog box, select the **Display** tab, section Detail View Defaults/ Window select *Floating* (see page 28), so that an item window is always opened in undocked mode.

Any window can be closed in a usual way by clicking on the upper rightmost cross and all windows can be closed by going to **View | Workspace | Close All**.

Ribbons

NVivo 9 introduces Windows-style Ribbons, replacing both menus and toolbars.

As the ribbon tabs take up a lot of space on the screen it is often a good idea to hide them when they are not needed. Hiding tabs is done by clicking the small arrow on the **Quick Access Toolbar**:

Select the options *Show Above the Ribbon* and *Minimize the Ribbon*. The menu tabs are shown again as soon as you point at any menu alternative. The menu tabs are:

The **Home** tab:

The **Create** tab:

The **External Data** tab:

The **Analyze** tab:

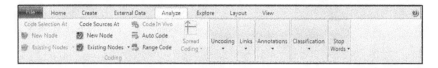

The **Explore** tab:

The **Layout** tab:

The **View** tab:

The following tabs are available depending on the Project Item type that is open:

The **Media** tab:

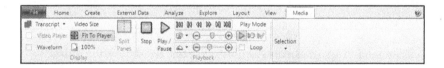

The **Picture** tab:

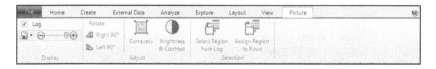

The **Chart** tab:

The **Model** tab:

The **Cluster Analysis** tab:

The **Tree Map** tab:

The **Word Tree** tab:

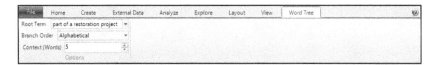

The **Graph** tab:

The guidelines of this book have adopted the following rules when referring to any command using the ribbon tabs:
For example:
Go to **Model | Shapes | Change Shape** represents:

- **Model** tab
- Tab group **Shapes**
- Tab option **Change Shape**

Options

Settings in **Applications Options** are not always effectuated in the current project. Most of the settings will instead be inherited in the project template and will be included in **Project Properties** next time a new project is created. When Project Properties are modified then the settings are taking effect instantly.

♦   **Follow These Steps**
  1   Go to **File → Options**.

Within the **Application Options** dialog box, select the **General** tab:

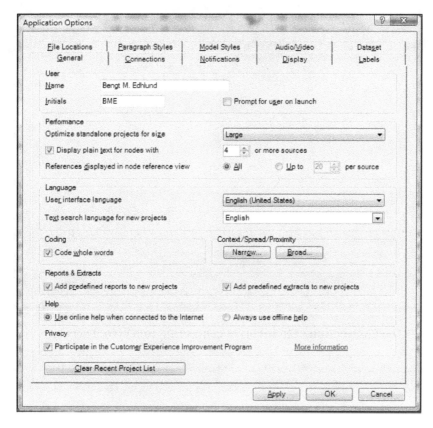

Under the **General** tab, you can change current user and language (interface and text search). It is recommended to set **Optimize standalone projects for size** *Large* which allocates more resources to NVivo. Any new settings, once applied, take effect next time you open a project.

Display plain text for nodes with *<value>* **or more sources** ensures better performance for large projects. *<value>* should be as low as possible. You can restore the source fonts and text attributes by going to **View | Detail View | Node → Rich Text**.

Within the **Application Options** dialog box, select the **Connections** tab:

The **Connections** tab involves connecting to NVivo 9 Server.

Within the **Application Options** dialog box, select the **Notifications** tab:

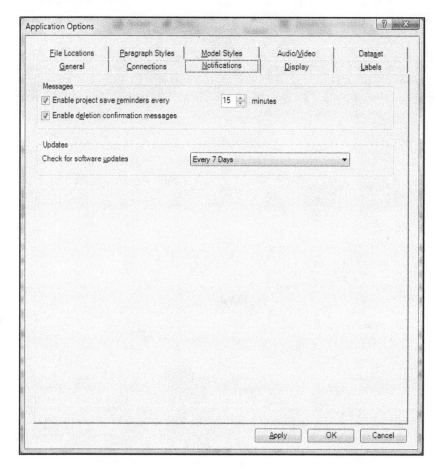

Under the **Notifications** tab, we recommend that a save reminder displays every 10 or 15 minutes and that you activate **Check for software updates** *Every 7 Days*.

Within the **Application Options** dialog box, select the **Display** tab:

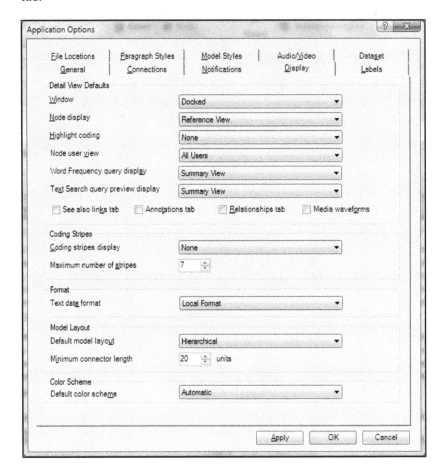

The **Display** tab defines default settings for certain functions. The maximum number of coding stripes can be set between 7 and 200. This setting takes immediate effect and applies to all NVivo projects. The setting can be modified for a certain item by going to **View | Coding | Coding Stripes → Number of Stripes**.

Within the **Application Options** dialog box, select the **Labels** tab:

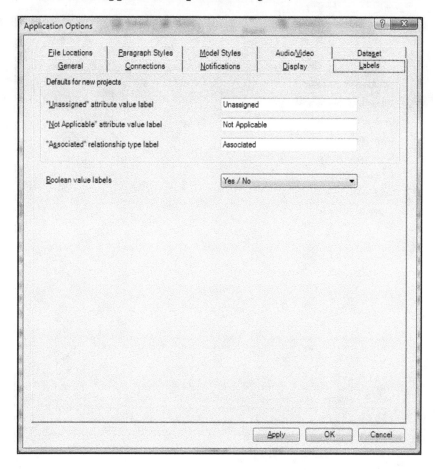

The **Labels** tab allows you to modify the names of certain labels.

Within the **Application Options** dialog box, select the **File Locations** tab:

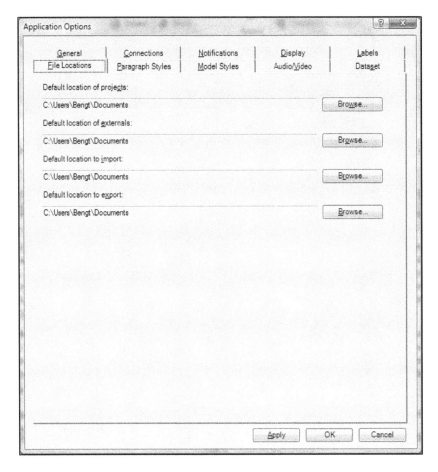

Under the **File Locations** tab you can change the file locations of projects, externals and the default locations of imported and exported project items and data.

Within the **Application Options** dialog box, select the
Paragraph Styles tab:

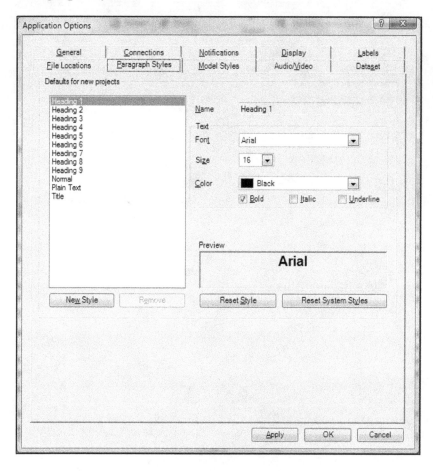

Fonts, font sizes, font attributes, and font colors for the given
paragraph styles are set under the **Paragraph Styles** tab. Changes
will be available next time a new project is created. Existing project
settings can be modified under the **Text Styles** tab in **Project
Properties** (see page 43).

Within the **Application Options** dialog box, select the **Model Styles** tab:

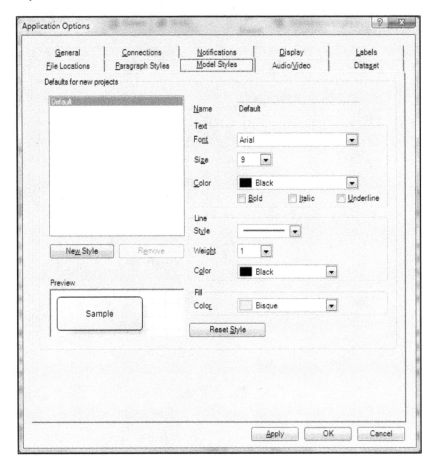

The **Model Styles** tab makes it possible to define fonts, line weight, style, color, and fill color for shapes in a model. You may create any set of new styles for existing projects. Changes made will be made available the next time a new project is created. The settings will be available under the **Models Styles** tab in **Project Properties** (see page 44), which in turn can be modified further for each project.

Within the **Application Options** dialog box, select the
Audio/Video tab:

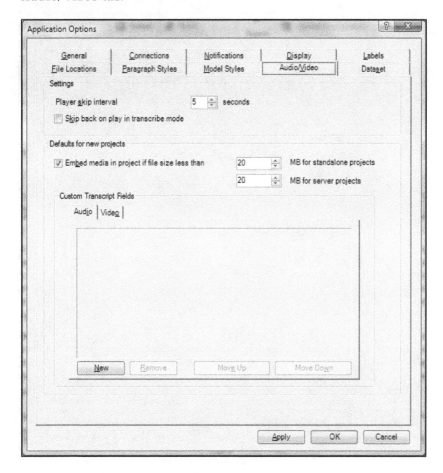

The **Audio/Video** tab contains settings for the skip interval for
skipping forward and skipping backward. These settings have an
immediateeffect on an open project. You can also create custom
transcript fields (or columns) for audio and video items. These fields
will come into existence for all new projects. For an existing project
go to **File → Project Properties**, and select the **Audio/Video** tab.

Settings for the threshold value of embedded audio and video files
are set under:

Embed media in project if file size less than <value> MB.

Within the **Application Options** dialog box, select the **Dataset** tab:

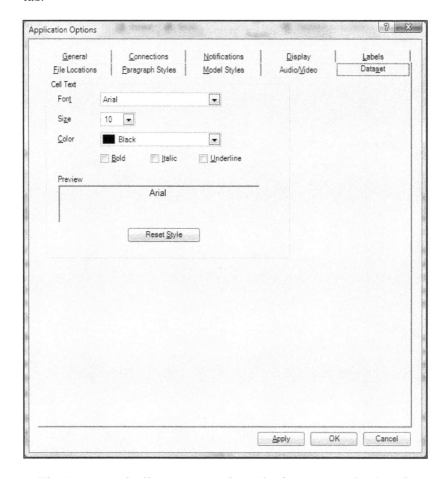

The **Dataset** tab allows you to adjust the font, size and color of cell text. Modifications made here will take effect next time a Dataset is opened.

Other Screen Settings

As an alternative screen the areas (**3**) and (**4**) can share screen space vertically in stead of horizontally.

♦ **Follow These Steps**

1 Go to **View | Workspace | Detail View → Right**.

This setting can be very handy when you are coding with drag-and-drop.

Revert to original setting of the screen:

♦ **Follow These Steps**

1 Go to **View | Workspace | Detail View → Bottom**.

The **Right Detail View** setting only applies during the current work session and cannot be saved.

- ♦ -

For more screen space it is also possible to temporarily close areas **(1)** and **(2)**.

♦ **Follow These Steps**

1 Go to **View | Workspace → Navigation View**

or key command **[Alt] + [F1]**, which is a toggling function.

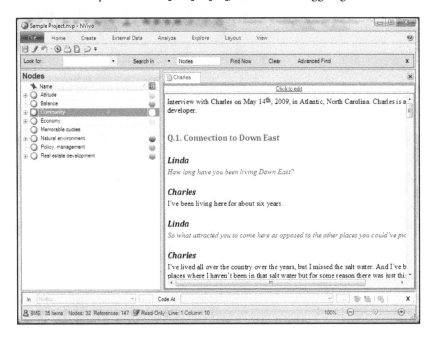

This setting is saved during current session even if you open another project. You can navigate to other folders by going to **Home | Workspace | Go key → <select>** or key commands like **[Ctrl] + [1]** and so on. Each time NVivo is started the Navigation View is restored.

3. CREATING A PROJECT

An NVivo project is a term used for all source documents and other items that altogether form a qualitative study. A project is also a computer file that houses all those project items.

NVivo can only open and process one project at a time. It is however possible to start the program twice and open one project in each program window. Cut, copy, and paste between two such program windows is limited to text, graphics and images and not project items like documents or nodes.

A project is built up of several items with different properties. There are internal sources (i.e., documents, memos), external sources (i.e., web sites), nodes and queries.

Creating a New Project

The NVivo welcome screen looks like this:

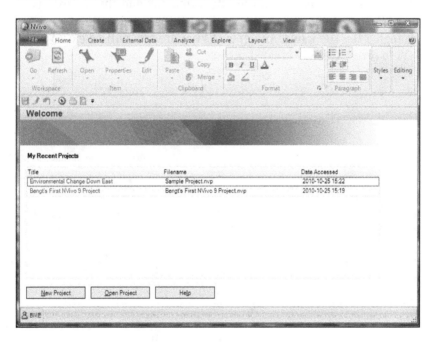

The most recent projects are listed on the welcome screen. The [**New Project**] button makes it possible to create a new project. *Alternatively*, you can also create a new project while navigating inside the program

♦ **Follow These Steps**

1   Go to **File → New**
     or key command [**Ctrl**] + [**N**].

The **New Project** dialog box now appears:

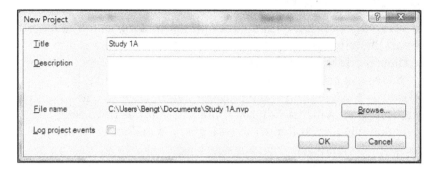

2 Type a name (compulsory) and a description (optional), then [**OK**].

The default location of the project file is determined in the **Application Options** dialog box, the **File Locations** tab (see page 30). The file path is seen in the **File name** box and the file extension is .NVP. The name of a project can later be changed without changing the file name. Any open NVivo projects will be closed as NVivo opens a newly created project.

Project Properties

When a new project is created some settings defined in the **Application Options** dialog box are inherited. This dialog box opens by going to **File → Options**, and the settings that are inherited are found under these tabs: **Labels**, **Paragraph Styles, Model Styles**, and **Audio/Video**. Modifications and new templates which are done in the **Project Properties** dialog box are only valid for the current project.

◆ **Follow These Steps**

1   Go to **File → Info → Project Properties**.

The **Project Properties** dialog box now appears select the **General** tab:

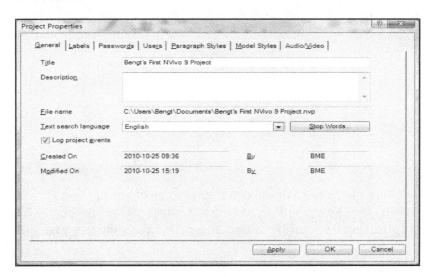

In this dialog box it is possible to modify the project name, but not the file name. From the **Text Search Language** drop-down list you will, if available, select the language of the data used in the project, otherwise select *English* or *None*. Search language is important when using Text Search Queries and Word Frequency Queries. A list of stop words is built in for certain languages. The list with stop words can be edited with the button [**Stop Words**], and this also works for the language setting *None*. Customized stop words are only valid for the current project. The list of stop words can be extende while using Text Search Queries and Word Frequency Queries (see Chapter 15, About Queries).

The Description (max 512 characters) can be modified. *Log project events* is optional.

Within the **Project Properties** dialog box, select the **Labels** tab:

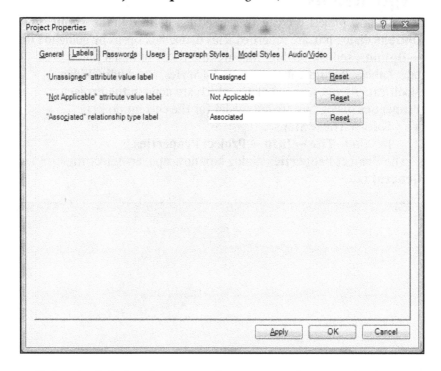

Under the **Labels** tab you can change some of your project's 'labels'. The [**Reset**] buttons reset to the values defined in the **Application Options** dialog box, under the **Labels** tab (see page 29).

Within the **Project Properties** dialog box, select the **Passwords** tab:

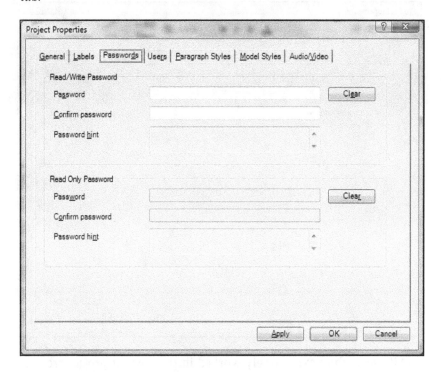

Under the **Passwords** tab you can define separate passwords for opening and editing the current project.

Within the **Project Properties** dialog box, select the **Users** tab:

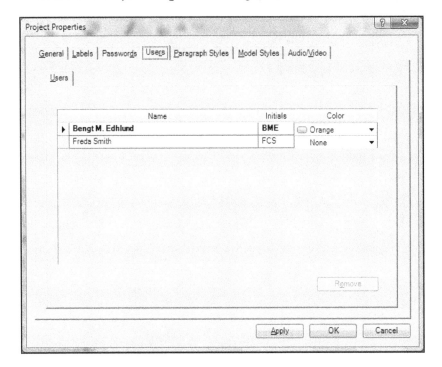

All users who have actively worked in the current project are listed here. The current user is identified by bold letters. You can replace a user with someone else on the list by selecting the user who shall be replaced (triangle) and using the [**Remove**] button. Select who will replace the deleted user by selecting from the list of users.

Users can also be given an individual color marking. Use the drop down list in the Color column and select color. This color marking can be used when viewing coding stripes per user.

Within the **Project Properties** dialog box, select the **Paragraph Styles** tab:

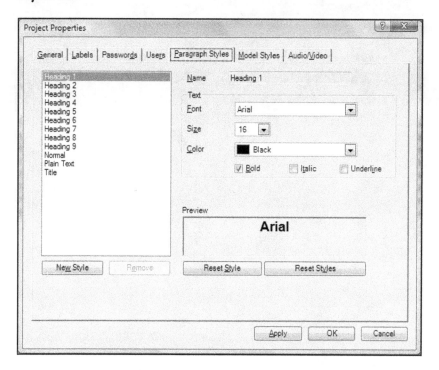

Under the **Paragraph Styles** tab, you can redefine your paragraph styles. The [**Reset Styles**] buttons reset to values defined in the **Application Options** dialog box (see page 31).

Within the **Project Properties** dialog box, select the **Model Styles** tab:

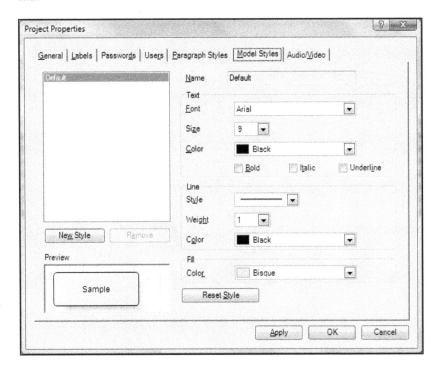

When a new project is created, NVivo retains the styles that were previously defined with the **Application Options** dialog box, under the **Model Styles** tab (see page 32). New styles created in the **Project Properties** dialog box are only valid for the current project.

Within the **Project Properties** dialog box, select the **Audio/Video** tab:

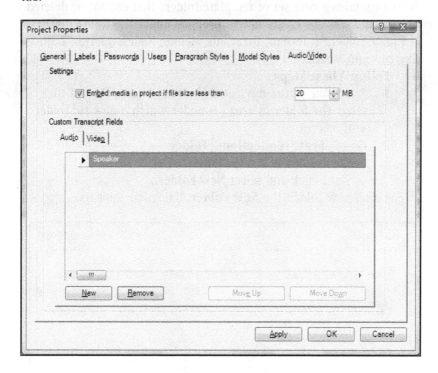

The settings for new projects are inherited from the **Application Options** dialog box, the **Audio/Video** tab (see page 32). Modifications made here are only valid for the current project.

Creating New Folder

NVivo contains a core set of template folders that cannot be deleted or moved. Users can create new subfolders under the following template folders: Internals, Externals, Memos, Nodes, Queries, Reports, Extracts and Models.

♦ **Follow These Steps**
  1 Select one of the navigation buttons in area **(1)** and then select the folder in area **(2)** under which a new subfolder will be created.
  2 Go to **Create | Collections | Folder**
    or key command **[Ctrl] + [Shift] + [N]**
    or right-click and select **New Folder...**

For each new folder, the **New Folder** dialog box appears:

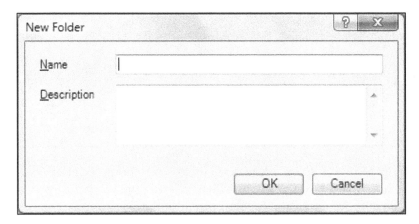

  3 Type a name (compulsory) and a descripton (optional), then **[OK]**.

Deleting a Folder

♦ **Follow These Steps**
  1 Select the folder or folders in area **(2)** that you want to delete.
  2 Use the **[Del]** key
    or go to **Home | Editing | Delete**
    or right-click and select **Delete**.
  3 Confirm with **[Yes]**.

Creating New Sets

Sets are defined as folders under the parent folder **Sets** that contains shortcuts to various project items or groups of project items. A set is considered a subset or collection of project items that allow you to access organized groups of items without moving or copying those items. A set cannot have subfolders.

♦ **Follow These Steps**

1 Go to [**Folders**] or [**Collections**] in area **(1)**.
2 Select the **Sets** folder in area **(2)**.
3 Go to **Create | Collections | Sets**
   or key command [**Ctrl**] + [**Shift**] + [**N**]
   or right-click and select **New Set...**

The **New Set** dialog box now appears:

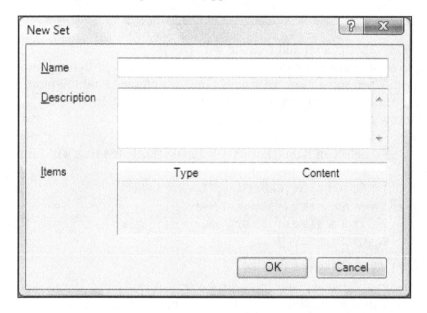

4 Type a name (compulsory) and a description (optional), then [**OK**].

Next, you need to define the members of your set.

♦ **Follow These Steps**

1 Select the item or items that will form a set.
2 Go to **Create | Collections | Add To Set**
   or right-click and select **Add To Set...**

The **Select Set** dialog box now appears:

3   Select a set and confirm with [**OK**].

You select items or shortcuts from any folder and paste them into a set. When using **Find**, **Advanced Find**, or **Grouped Find** the result can easily be added to a set. Sets can be used as an alternative to storing results in a subfolder to **Search Folders**.

♦   **Follow These Steps**
1   Select an item (shortcut) or items (shortcuts) that will form a new set.
2   Go to **Create | Collections | Create As Set**.

The **New Set** dialog box now appears.

3   Type a name of the new set.
4   Confirm with [**OK**].

Copying, Cutting and Pasting

The usual Windows conventions for copy, cut, and paste prevail in NVivo. In addition NVivo can also copy, cut, and paste complete project items like documents, memos, nodes, etc. However, it is not possible to paste nodes into folders meant for documents and vice versa. It is only possible to paste an item into the folder appropriate for that type of folder.

♦   **Follow These Steps**
1   Select an item (document, node etc.)
2   Go to **Home | Clipboard | Cut**
     or key command [**Ctrl**] + [**X**]
     or right-click and select **Cut**.

alternatively

2   Go to **Home | Clipboard | Copy**
     or key command [**Ctrl**] + [**C**]
     or right-click and select **Copy**.

3   Select the approptriate folder or parent node under which you want to place the item.

4   Go to **Home | Clipboard | Paste → Paste**
    or key command **[Ctrl] + [V]**
    or right-click and select **Paste**.

Paste Special

The normal **Paste** command includes all those elements. But after copying or cutting of some items (excluding nodes) you can decide which elements from the item that should be pasted.

♦   **Follow These Steps**

1   Copy or cut the item or items that you want to paste into the new position.

2   Select the target folder.

3   Go to **Home | Clipboard | Paste → Paste Special...**

The **Paste Special Options** dialog box now appears:

4   Select the item elements that you want to include. The options *Media content* and *Transcript* are valid for video and audio items and *Log entries* is valid for picture items.

5   Confirm with **[OK]**.

Merging Nodes

Any node can be merged into an existing node.

♦ **Follow These Steps**

1 Cut or copy one or more node(s).

2 Select a target node.

3 Go to **Home | Clipboard | Merge → Merge Into Selected Node**
or key command **[Ctrl] + [M]**
or right-click and select **Merge Into Selected Node**.

In each case the **Merge Into Node** dialog box appears:

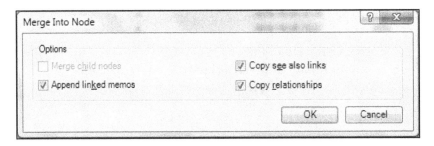

4 Select the applicable options, then click **[OK]**.

Alternatively, you can merge two (or more) nodes into a new node.

♦ **Follow These Steps**

1 Cut or copy two or more nodes.

2 Select the folder or parent node under which you want to place the nodes in your clipboard.

3 Click on any empty space in area **(3)**.

4 Go to **Home | Clipboard | Merge → Merge Into New Node...**
or right-click and select **Merge Into New Node...**

alternatively

4 Go to **Home | Clipboard | Merge → Merge Into New Child Node**
or right-click and select **Merge Into New Child Node...**

The **Merge Into Node** dialog box now appears:

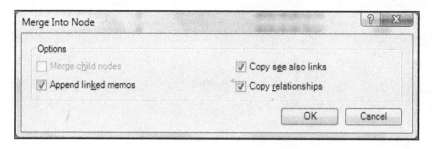

5 Select the applicable option(s), then click [**OK**].
The **New Node** dialog box now appears:

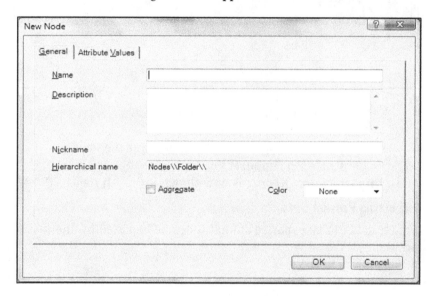

6   Type name (compulsory) and description and Nickname
    (optional), then [**OK**].

Merging Projects

Projects can be merged by importing one project to another.
♦   **Follow These Steps**
    1   Open the project into which you wish to import a project.
    2   Go to **External Data | Import | Project**.

The **Import Project** dialog box now appears:

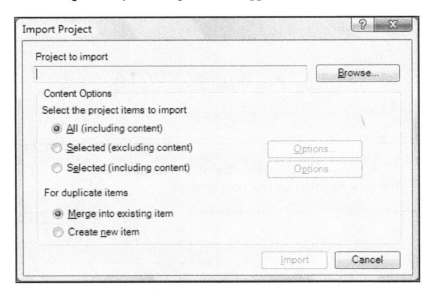

3   The [**Browse...**] button opens a file browser. Search for the
project file to be imported.

4   Select the item options that you need for the import.

5   Confirm with [**Import**].

An **Import Project Report** is now shown listing all items.

Exporting Project Data

Project data can be exported so that it can be imported by another
project.

♦   **Follow These Steps**

1   Open a project.

2   Go to **External Data | Export | Export → Project...**

The **Export Project Data** dialog box now appears:

At **Export items** and the [**Select**] button you decide what items
that shall be exported and at **Export to** and the [**Specify**] button
you decide the name and location of the exported project data.

Save and Security Backup

You can save the project file at any time during a work session. The complete project is saved; it is not possible to save single project items.

♦ **Follow These Steps**
  1 Go to **File → Save**
    or key command **[Ctrl] + [S]**.

If the option *Enable project save reminders every 15 minutes* has been chosen (see page 27) the following message will appear:

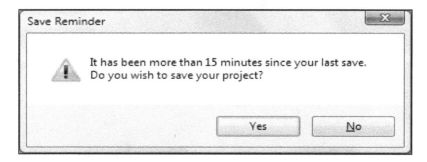

2 Confirming with **[Yes]** saves the whole project file.

Security backup is easy since the whole project is one file and not a structure of files and folders. Use Windows native tools for backup copies and follow the backup routines that your organization applies. The command **File → Manage → Copy Project** creates a copy of the project at the location that you decide while the current project remains.

Undo

The undo-function can be made in several steps back and forth. Undo only works for commands made after the last save.

♦ **Follow These Steps**
  1 Go to **Undo** on the **Quick Access Toolbar**
    or key command **[Ctrl] + [Z]**.

The arrow next to the undo-icon makes it possible to select which of the last five commands that shall be undone. When you select the first option only the last command is undone and when you select the last option all commands will be undone.

The option **Redo** (Undo – Undo) is available in Word but not in NVivo.

4. HANDLING TEXT-SOURCES

Documents

Source items can be imported from sources created outside NVivo like Word documents. Source items can also be created by NVivo as most word processing tools and functions are incorporated in NVivo software.

Importing Documents

This section is about text-based sources that can be imported and these file types are: .DOC, .DOCX, .RTF, .TXT, and .PDF. When the documents have been imported they will become items in an NVivo project. A PDF-document that have been imported will be converted to an item similar to a Word document and can be edited, coded and linked as any other item.

PDF-documents with a lot of graphics and an advanced column structure may lose some of their original layout when converted by NVivo. The solution in this case is to first convert the PDF to a Word document with the software Acrobat Professional or Fine Reader and then import it or to create an External item with a link to the PDF-document (see page 60).

♦ **Follow These Steps**
1 Go to **External Data | Import | Documents**
   Default folder is **Internals**.
   Go to 5.
alternatively
1 Click on [**Sources**] in area **(1)**.
2 Select the **Internals** folder in area **(2)** or its subfolder.
3 Go to **External Data | Import | Documents**
   or key command [**Ctrl**] + [**Shift**] + [**I**]
   Go to 5.
alternatively
3 Click on any empty space in area **(3)**.
4 Right click and select **Import Internals → Import Documents...**

In each case, the **Import Internals** dialog box appears:

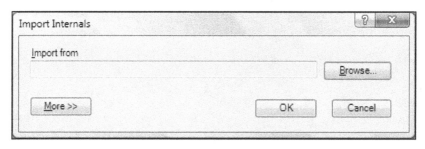

5   The [**Browse...**] button gives access to a filebrowser and you can select one or several documents for a batch import.

6   When the documents have been selected, confirm with [**Open**].

The [**More** >>] button offers several options:

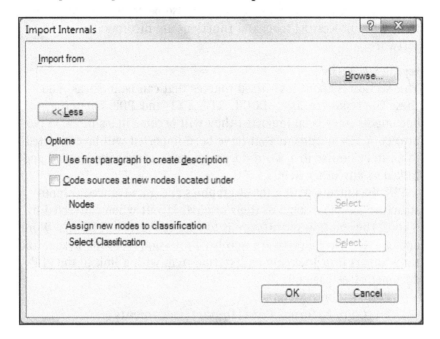

Use first paragraph to create descriptions. NVivo copies the first paragraph of the document and pastes it into the descriptions text box.

Code sources at new nodes located under. Each source item will be coded at a node with the same name as the imported file and located under the folder and parent node that has been selected. Also you must assign the nodes to a Classification when importing (see page 130 about Classification Sheets).

7   Confirm the import with [**OK**].

When only *one* document has been imported the **Document Properties** dialog box appears:

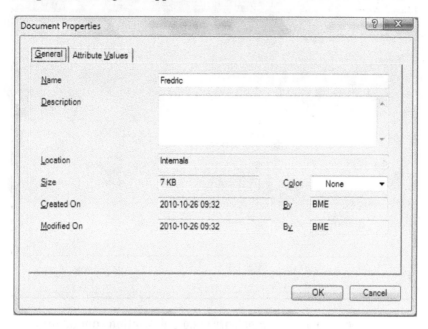

This dialog box will make it possible to modify the name of the item and optionally add a description.

8   Confirm with [**OK**].

All documents and other items are Write Only each time they are opened. Therefore they must be set to an edit mode when you need to make changes or additions. Coding and linking however (but not hyperlinking), can be made in a Write Only mode.

Creating a New Document

♦ **Follow These Steps**

1   Go to **Create | Sources | Document**
Default folder is **Internals**.
Go to 5.

alternatively

1   Click on [**Sources**] in area (**1**).
2   Select the **Internals** folder in area (**2**) or its subfolder.
3   Go to **Create | Sources | Document**
or key command [**Ctrl**] + [**Shift**] + [**N**].
Go to 5.

alternatively

3   Click on any empty space in area (**3**).
4   Right-click and select **New Internal → New Document...**

The **New Document** dialog box now appears:

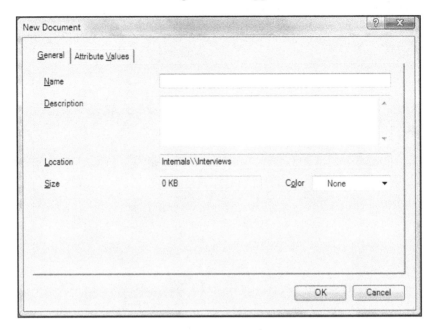

5   Type a name (compulsory) and a desription (optionally), then [**OK**].

Here is a typical list view in area (**3**) of some source items:

Opening a Document

◆   **Follow These Steps**
1   Click on [**Sources**] in area (**1**).
2   Select the **Internals** folder in area (**2**) or its subfolder.
3   Select the document in area (**3**) that you want to open.
4   Go to **Home | Item | Open**
or key command [**Ctrl**] + [**Shift**] + [**O**]
or right-click and select **Open Document...**
or double-click on the document in area (**3**).

Please note, you can only open one document at a time, but several documents can stay open simultaneously.

Exporting Documents

♦ **Follow These Steps**

1 Click [**Sources**] in area **(1)**.
2 Select the **Internals** folder in area **(2)** or its subfolder.
3 Select the document or documents in area **(3)** that you want to export.
4 Go to **External Data | Export | Export → Export Document...**
  or key command [**Ctrl**] + [**Shift**] + [**E**]
  or right-click and select **Export → Export Document...**

The **Export Options** dialog box now appears:

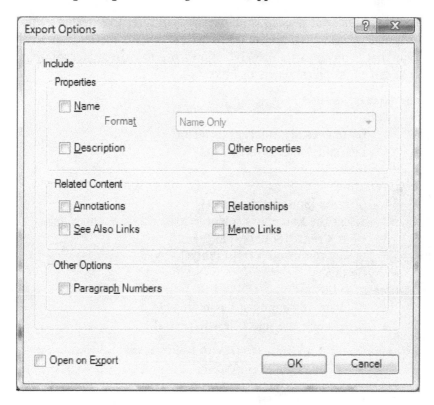

5 Select the options that you want. Confirm with [**OK**].
6 Decide file name, file location, and file type. Possible file types are: .DOCX, .DOC, .RTF, .TXT, .PDF, or .HTML. Confirm with [**Save**].

Please note, that any coding made on such items cannot be transferred when a source item is exported.

- **Follow These Steps**
  1   Click on [**Sources**] in area (**1**).
  2   Select the **Internals** folder in area (**2**) or its subfolder.
  3   Select the document or documents in area (**3**) that you want to delete.
  4   Go to **Home** | **Editing** | **Delete**
      or use [**Del**] key
      or right-click and select **Delete**.
  5   Confirm with [**Yes**].

External Items

For any number of reasons, you may wish to refer to external items outside of your NVivo project (i.e., a web site, a file too large or a file type that is incompatible). NVivo allows you to create external items that can act as placeholders or links.

Creating an External Item
- **Follow These Steps**
  1   Go to **Create** | **Sources** | **External**
      Deafault folder is **Externals**.
      Go to 5.

  alternatively
  1   Click on [**Sources**] in area (**1**).
  2   Select the **Externals** folder in area (**2**) or its subfolder.
  3   Go to **Create** | **Sources** | **External**
      or key command [**Ctrl**] + [**Shift**] + [**N**].
      Go to 5.

  alternatively
  3   Click on any empty space in area (**3**).
  4   Right-click and select **New External...**

The **New External** dialog box now appears:

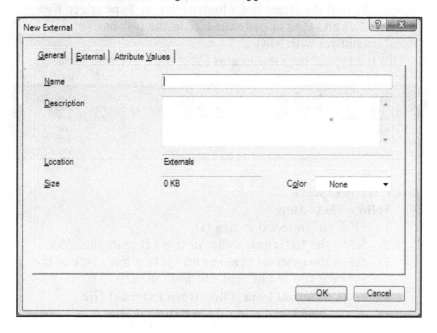

5   Type name (compulsory) and description (optional), then go
     to the **External** tab.

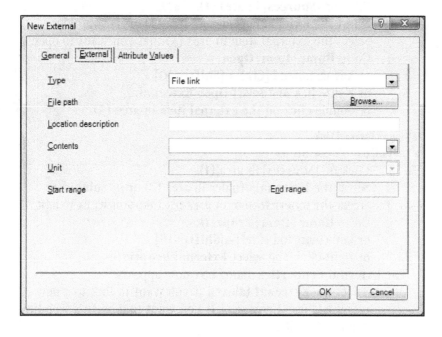

6   At **Type** select *File link* and then use the [Browse...] button
      to find the target file. Alternatively, at **Type** select *Web
      link* and type or paste the URL in the text box below.
7   Confirm with [**OK**].

This is a typical list view in area **(3)** of some external items:

Externals							
Name	Nodes	References	Created On	Created By	Modified On	Modified By	
Reference Instructions	0	0	2010-10-27 16:	BME	2010-10-27 16:4	BME	
Guidelines	0	0	2010-10-27 16:	BME	2010-10-27 16:4	BME	
Literature Listing	0	0	2010-10-27 16:	BME	2010-10-27 16:4	BME	
Article on Methods	0	0	2010-10-27 16:	BME	2010-10-27 16:4	BME	

Opening an External Source

♦   **Follow These Steps**
1   Click on [**Sources**] in area **(1)**.
2   Select the **Externals** folder in area **(2)** or its subfolder.
3   Select the external item in area **(3)** that has a link to the
      external file or URL that you want to open.
4   Go to **External Data | Files | Open External File**
      or right-click and select **Open External File**.

Opening an External Item

♦   **Follow These Steps**
1   Click on [**Sources**] in area **(1)**.
2   Select the **Externals** folder in area **(2)** or its subfolder.
3   Select the external item in area **(3)** that you want to open.
4   Go to **Home | Item | Open**
      or key command [**Ctrl**] + [**Shift**] + [**O**]
      or right-click and select **Open External...**
      or double-click on the external item in area **(3)**.

Editing an External Link

♦   **Follow These Steps**
1   Click on [**Sources**] in area **(1)**.
2   Select the **Externals** folder in area **(2)** or its subfolder.
3   Select the external item in area **(3)** that you want to edit.
4   Go to **Home | Item | Properties**
      or key command [**Ctrl**] + [**Shift**] + [**P**]
      or right-click and select **External Properties...**

The **External Properties** dialog box now appears.
5   Select the **External** tab and if you want to link to a new
      target file use [**Browse...**]. If you want to modify a web link
      change the URL.

♦ **Follow These Steps**

1 Click on [**Sources**] in area (**1**).
2 Select the **Externals** folder in area (**2**) or its subfolder.
3 Select the external item or items in area (**3**) that you want to export.
4 Go to **External Data | Export | Export**
   or key command [**Ctrl**] + [**Shift**] + [**E**]
   or right-click and select **Export → Export External...**

The **Export Options** dialog box now appears.

5 Select the options that you want. Confirm with [**OK**].
6 Decide file name, file location, and file type. Possible file types are: .DOCX, .DOC, .RTF, .TXT, .PDF, or .HTML. Confirm with [**Save**].

The linked external file or the web link is not included in the exported item, only the contents of the external item is.

♦ **Follow These Steps**

1 Click on [**Sources**] in area (**1**).
2 Select the **Externals** folder in area (**2**) or its subfolder.
3 Select the external item or items in area (**3**) that you want to delete.
4 Go to **Home | Editing | Delete**
   or use the [**Del**] key
   or right-click and select **Delete**.
5 Confirm with [**Yes**].

5. EDITING DOCUMENTS IN NVIVO

Whether you import a document or create a new one in NVivo you have access to most of the editing options of a modern word processor.

Each time a source item is opened it is Read Only. Therefore you need to click on the link *Click to edit* at the top of a source item window before you can edit. Alternatively, you can go to **Home | Item | Edit** which is a toggling function. You can code and create links (but not hyperlinks) in a Read Only source item.

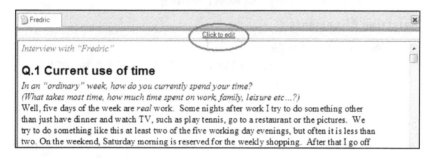

Fonts, Font Style, Size, and Color

◆ **Follow These Steps**
1   Select the text you want to format.
2   Go to **Home | Format → Font...**
The **Font** dialog box now appears:

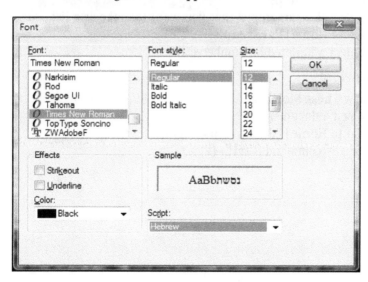

3   Select the options you need and confirm with [**OK**].

Selecting a Style

♦ **Follow These Steps**
1 Position the cursor in the paragraph you want to format.
2 Go to **Home | Styles**.
3 Select from the list of styles.
4 Confirm with **[OK]**.

Reset to previous style is possible as long as the project has not been saved after the last change.

♦ **Follow These Steps**
1 Position the cursor in the paragraph you want to reset.
2 Go to **Home | Styles | Reset Settings**.

Selecting Alignments

♦ **Follow These Steps**
1 Position the cursor in the paragraph you want to format.
2 Go to **Home | Paragraph**.
3 Select from the list of alignment options.

Selecting Indentation

♦ **Follow These Steps**
1 Position the cursor in the paragraph for which you want to change the indentation.
2 Go to **Home | Paragraph**.
3 Select increased or decreased indentation.

Creating Lists

♦ **Follow These Steps**
1 Select the paragraphs that you want to make as a list.
2 Go to **Home | Paragraph**.
3 Select a bulleted or numbered list.

Searching Words

♦ **Follow These Steps**
1 Open a document.
2 Go to **Home | Editing | Find → Find...**
or key command **[Ctrl] + [F]**.

The **Find Content** dialog box now appears:

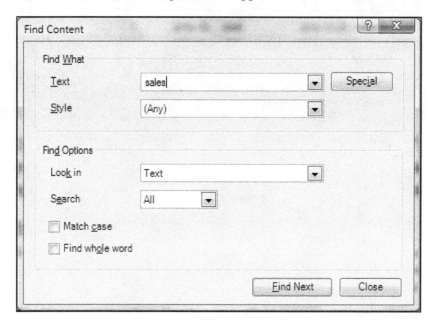

3   Type a search word, then click [**Find Next**].

The **Style** option makes it possible to limit the search from *Any* to a certain style.

Please note the option *Match case* which makes it possible to exactly match *UPPERCASE* or *lowercase* and the option *Find whole word* which switches off the free text search.

Searching and Replacing

♦   **Follow These Steps**

1   Open a document.

2   Go to **Home | Editing | Replace**
     or key command [**Ctrl**] + [**H**].

The **Replace Content** dialog box now appears:

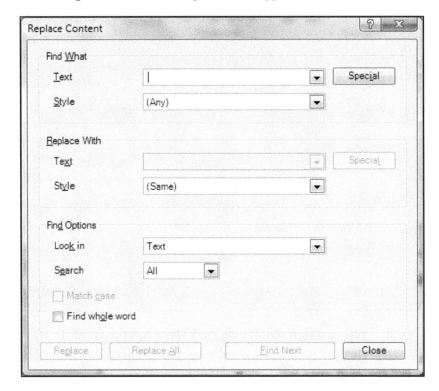

3 Type a find word and a replace word, then [**Replace**] or
   [**Replace All**].

The option *Style* near **Find What** makes it possible limit the
search from *All* to any given style and the option *Style* near **Replace
With** makes it possible to replace the found word as well as change
the style from *Same* to any given style.

Please notice the option *Match case* which makes it possible to
exactly match *UPPERCASE* and *lowercase* and the option *Find whole
word* which switches off the doublesided autotruncation.

Selecting Text

Selecting text: Click and drag
Selecting one word: Double-click
Selecting a paragraph:

♦ **Follow These Steps**

1 Position the cursor in the paragraph you want to select.

2 Go to **Home | Editing | Select → Select Paragraph**
   or triple-click.

Selecting the whole document:

♦ **Follow These Steps**

1   Position the cursor anywhere in the documen.
2   Go to **Home | Editing | Select→ Select All**
     or key command **[Ctrl] + [A]**.

Go to a Certain Position

♦ **Follow These Steps**

1   Go to **Home | Editing | Find → Go to ...**
     or key command **[Ctrl] + [G]**.

The **Go to** dialog box now appears:

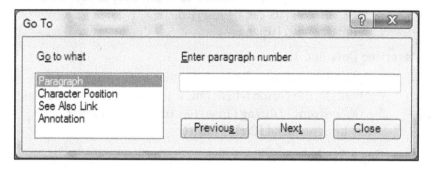

2   Select option at **Go to what** and when required, a value.
3   Click on **[Previous]** or **[Next]**.

Creating a Table

♦ **Follow These Steps**

1   Position the cursor where you want to create a table.
2   Go to **Home | Editing | Insert → Insert Text Table...**

The **Insert Text Table** dialog box now appears:

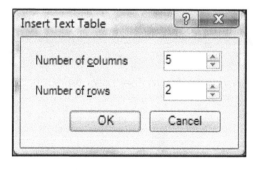

3   Select number of columns and number of rows in the table.
4   Confirm with **[OK]**.

Inserting Page Break

♦ **Follow These Steps**
1 Position the cursor where you want to insert a page break.
2 Go to **Home | Editing | Insert → Insert Page Break**.

A page break is indicated with a dotted line on the screen.

Inserting an Image

♦ **Follow These Steps**
1 Position the cursor where you want to insert an image.
2 Go to **Home | Editing | Insert → Insert Image...**
3 Select an image with the file browser. Only .BMP, .JPG and .GIF file formats can be inserted.
4 Confirm with [**Open**].

Inserting Date and Time

♦ **Follow These Steps**
1 Position the cursor where you want to insert date and time.
2 Go to **Home | Editing | Insert → Insert Date/Time**
or key command [**Ctrl**] + [**Shift**] + [**T**].

Inserting a Symbol

♦ **Follow These Steps**
1 Position the cursor where you want to insert a symbol.
2 Go to **Home | Editing | Insert → Insert Symbol**
or key command [**Ctrl**] + [**Shift**] + [**Y**].
3 Select a symbol from the **Insert Symbol** dialog box, confirm with [**Insert**].

Zooming

♦ **Follow These Steps**
1 Open a document.
2 Go to **View | Zoom | Zoom | Zoom...**

The **Zoom** dialog box appears:

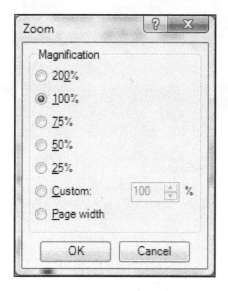

3   Select a certain magnification and confirm with [**OK**].
Alternatively, you may also use the Zoom-slider in the status bar below on the screen.
Alternatively, [**Ctrl**] + your mouse wheel allows zooming in or out.
You can also zoom in or out in predetermined steps:
♦   **Follow These Steps**
1   Open a document.
2   Go to **View** | **Zoom** | **Zoom** | **Zoom In**
or **View** | **Zoom** | **Zoom** | **Zoom Out**.

Print Previewing

♦   **Follow These Steps**
1   Open a document.
2   Go to **File → Print → Print Preview**.

The **Print Options** dialog box now appears:

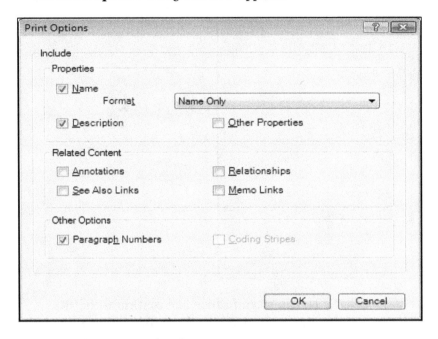

    3   Select options for the preview.
    4   Confirm with **[OK]**.

As you can see from the dialog box we have seleced the options *Name*, *Description* and *Paragraph Numbers*. This can be of great importance when working in a team. Also the page breaks are shown here and they are not on the screen.

The result can look like this:

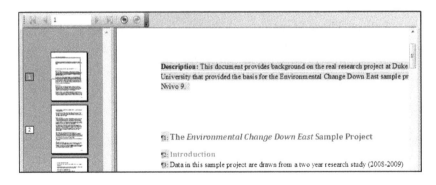

In the Print Preview window there are numerous possibilities to navigate, zoom, and change the view. The thumbnails can be hidden with **View → Thumbnails** which is a toggling function. Print all pages with **File → Print** or key command **[Ctrl]** + **[P]**.

Printing a Document

♦ **Follow These Steps**

1   Open a document.
2   Go to **File → Print → Print...**
    or key command **[Ctrl]** + **[P]**.
3   The **Print Options** dialog box (same as above) now appears. Select options for the printout.
4   Confirm with **[OK]**.

Printing with Coding Stripes

When you need to print a document with coding stripes (see page 166), you must first show the coding stripes on the screen. Then you need to select the option *Coding Stripes* in the **Print Options** dialog box:

The printout is made with the content of the document and the coding stripes on separate sheets:

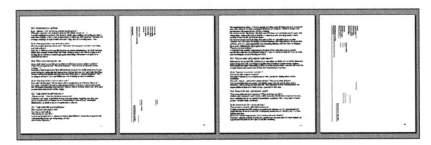

If you would like to have the document and the coding stripes on the same sheet you can set the printer to print *two pages on same sheet*. Set up for this option varies by printer, but can usually be found under the print properties dialog box. Printing in this manner is optimized by printing to legal or ledger stationary.

Page Setup

♦ **Follow These Steps**

   1   Open a document and open **Print Preview**.

   2   Go to **File → Page Setup...**

The **Page Setup** dialog box now appears:

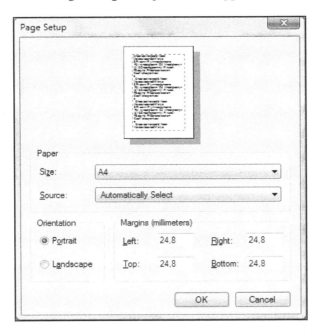

   3   Decide the settings for paper size, orientation and margins, then [**OK**].

Limitations in Editing Documents in NVivo

NVivo has certain limitations in creating advanced formatted documents.

Some of these limitations are:

- NVivo cannot merge two documents by any other means than copying/cutting and pasting text.
- It is difficult to format an image (change size, orientation, move).
- It is difficult to format a table.
- It is difficult to format a paragraph (hanging indent, first line different, line spacing).
- Spell check is not included.
- Copying from a Word document to NVivo loses some paragraph formatting.
- Footnotes in a Word document are lost after importing to NVivo.
- Field codes do not exist in NVivo and these are converted to text after importing to NVivo.
- NVivo cannot apply several columns, except when used in a table. When a multi-column document is imported it is displayed on the screen as single column. The multi-column design is restored when such document is exported or printed.

Often it is better to create a document in Word and then import to NVivo. Word footnotes must however be replaced by NVivo Annotations. Most formatting and styles are intact after importing to NVivo, but they often cannot be further edited.

6. HANDLING AUDIO- AND VIDEO-SOURCES

The objective of importing audio and video files is twofold. First, such material includes additional information such as tone and stength of voice, temperament, body language etc. Second, some projects can save costs by using NVivo to annotate keywords and short comments with audio data.

NVivo 9 can import the following audio formats: .MP3, .WAV, and - WMA and the following video formats: .MPG, .MPEG, .MPE, .WMV, .AVI, .MOV, .QT, and .MP4. Media files less than 40 MB can be imported and embedded in the project. Files larger than 40 MB must be stored as external files, but can nevertheless be handled the same way as an embedded item. The threshold value for audio and video files that shall be stored as external files can be reduced for all new projects with **File → Options...**, select the **Audio/Video** tab, section **Default for new projects** (see page 33). To adjust values for the current project, use **File → Info → Project Properties...**, select the **Audio/Video** tab, section **Settings** (see page 45).

When you need to view all items that are not embedded go to [**Sources**] in area (**1**), select **Search Folders** and subfolder **All Sources Not Embedded** in area (**2**).

Importing Media Files

♦ **Follow These Steps**
   1   Go to **External Data | Import | Audios/Videos**
       Default folder is **Internals**.
       Go to 5.
alternatively
   1   Click [**Sources**] in area (**1**).
   2   Select the **Internals** folder in area (**2**) or its subfolder.
   3   Go to **External Data | Import | Audios/Videos**
       or key command [**Ctrl**] + [**Shift**] + [**I**].
       Go to 5.
alternatively
   3   Click on any empty space in area (**3**).
   4   Right-click and select **Import Internals → Import Audios.../Import Videos...**

The **Import Internals** dialog box now appears:

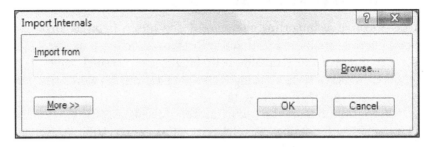

5   The [**Browse...**] button gives access to a filebrowser and you can select one or several media files for a batch import.

6   When the file or files have been chosen, confirm with [**Open**].

The [**More** >>] button lets you select more options:

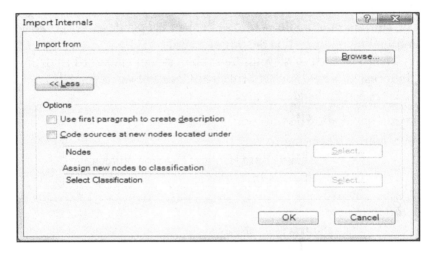

Use first paragraph to create descriptions. Not applicable for the import of media files.

Code sources at new nodes located under. Each source item will be coded at a node with the same name as the imported file and located under the folder and parent node that has been selected. Also you must assign the nodes to a Classification when importing. See page 130 about Classification Sheets.

7   Confirm the import with [**OK**].

When only one media file is imported the **Audio Properties/Video Properties** dialog box appears:

This dialog box will make it possible to modify the name of the item and optionally add a description. When the **Audio/Video** tab has been chosen you can let the audio file be stored as an external file even if the size is below the limit for embeding. After an audio- or video file has been imported you can change the properties from embedded item to external storage and vice versa by using **Audio Properties/Video Properties**. An embedded item cannot exceed 40 MB.

    8   Confirm with [**OK**].

At times you may need to move an external media file. When an external file has been moved the media item must be updated through NVivo. Go to **External Data | Files | Update File Location...** and select the external file's new location. From there, NVivo will find the correct media file.

Creating a New Media Item

♦   **Follow These Steps**
   1   Go to **Create | Sources | Audio/Video**.
       Default folder is **Internals**.
       Go to 5.
alternatively
   1   Click [**Sources**] in area (**1**).
   2   Select the **Internals** folder in area (**2**) or its subfolder.
   3   Go to **Create | Sources | Audio/Video**
       or key command [**Ctrl**] + [**Shift**] + [**N**].
       Go to 5.
alternatively
   3   Click on any empty space in area (**3**).
   4   Right-click and select **New Internal → New Audio.../New Video...**

The **New Audio/New Video** dialog box now appears:

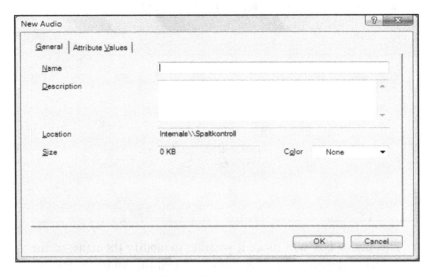

5 Type name (compulsory) and a description (optional), then [**OK**].

When you create a new media item it initially has no media file or transcript. Instead these pieces of information can be imported separately. From the open media item, click the **Edit Mode** link and go to **External Data | Import | Media Content** or **External Data | Import | Rows** (see page 84). From here, select the required contents.

Here is a typical list view in area (**3**) of some audio items:

Opening a Media Item

♦ **Follow These Steps**

1 Click [**Sources**] in area (**1**).

2 Select the **Internals** folder in area (**2**) or its subfolder.

3 Select the media item in area (**3**) that you want to open.

4 Go to **Home | Item | Open**
   or key command [**Ctrl**] + [**Shift**] + [**O**]
   or right-click and select **Open Audio/Video...**
   or double-click on the media item in area (**3**).

An open audio item may appear like this:

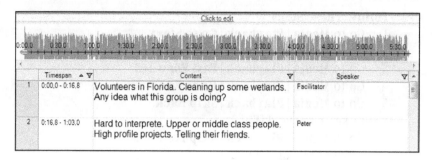

Provided a soundcard and speakers are connected to the computer you can now play and analyze the audio item.

Play Modes

Three play mode options are available: *Normal, Synchronize* or *Transcribe.*

Go to **Media | Playback | Playmode** to view or change playmode options.

Play, Stop

When a media item is opened the play mode is always *Normal.*

♦ **Follow These Steps**
1 Go to **Media | Playback | Play/Pause**
or key command [**F7**].

Only the selected section will be played if there is a selection along the timeline. The selection disappears when you click outside the selection.

2 Go to **Media | Playback | Stop**
or key command [**F8**].

Play Synchronized

You can play any media item synchronized so the text row is highlighted and always visible (by automatic scrolling).

♦ **Follow These Steps**
1 Go to **Media | Playback | Play Mode → Synchronize**.
2 Play.

Rewind, Fast Forward etc.

♦ **Follow These Steps**

1 Go to **Media | Playback | Go to Start**.
2 Go to **Media | Playback | Rewind**.
3 Go to **Media | Playback | Fast Forward**.
4 Go to **Media | Playback | Go to End**.
5 Go to **Media | Playback | Skip Back**.
   or key command [**F9**].
6 Go to **Media | Playback | Skip Forward**
   or key command [**F10**].

The *Skip* interval is determined by the setting under **File → Options**, the **Audio/Video** tab, see page 33.

Volume, Speed

♦ **Follow These Steps**

1 Go to **Media | Playback | Volume**. This slider also allows mute.
2 Go to **Media | Playback | Play Speed**. There are fixed positions and continuous slider.

About Transcripts

You can synchronize audio timeline intervals with text like written comments, direct transcripts or translations. First, define an interval that corresponds with the row of the table that accompanies the transcripts. Both the audio timeline interval and the transcript need to be coded and linked. Timeline intervals can be defined in a number of ways, such as by selecting portions of the timeline with your mouse or, while audio is playing, by entering certain commands that mark the beginning and end of an interval.

To make it easier to view a selection and other markings along the timeline you may wish to hide the waveform. Go to **Media | Display | Waveform**, which is a toggling function. Each media item retains its individual setting during the ongoing session.

You may set a default for viewing the waveform by going to **File → Options**, the **Display** tab and deselect *Waveform*.

Selecting along the Timeline – Play Mode Normal

♦ **Follow These Steps**

1   Use the left mousebutton to define the start of an interval, then hold the button, drag along the timeline, and release the button at the end of the interval.

alternatively

1   Play the media item, possibly at low speed, see above.

2   Determine the start of an interval by going to **Media | Selection | Start Selection** or key command [**F11**].

3   Determine the end of an interval by going to **Media | Selection | Stop Selection** or key command [**F12**].

The result is a selection (a blue frame) along the timeline. Now you can code or link from this selection. To proceed with creating the next selection you need to click outside the previous selection. Retaining the current selection will limit the play interval to that selection.

Creating a Transcript Row from a Time Slot

♦ **Follow These Steps**

1   Make a selection along the timeline.

2   Go to **Layout | Rows and Columns | Insert → Row** or key command [**Ctrl**] + [**Ins**].

The result is a transcript row corresponding to the selected time slot, *Timespan*, and the textbox is in the columns *Content*.

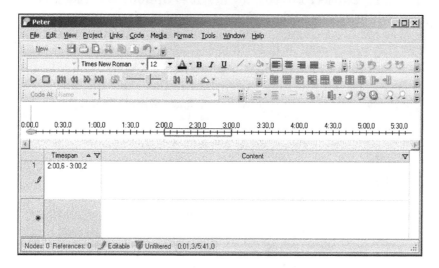

Should you need to adjust the timespan along a timeline you can do as follows:

♦ **Follow These Steps**

1 Select a transcript row by clicking in the row item number (the leftmost column). The corresponding timespan along the timeline is then marked with a purple guiding line.

2 Make a new modified selection along the timeline.

3 Go to **Media | Selection | Assign Timespan to Rows**.

As an alternative you can also modify the timespan directly in the transcript row by typing new start and stop coordinates. From there you can then make a new selection along the timeline.

♦ **Follow These Steps**

1 Select a transcript row by clicking in the row item number (the leftmost column).

2 Go to **Media | Selection | Select Media from Transcript**.

Creating a Transcript Row during Play - Play Mode Transcribe

♦ **Follow These Steps**

1 Go to **Media | Playback | Play Mode → Transcribe**.

2 Play and determine start of an interval by going to **Media | Playback | Start/Pause** or key command [**F7**].

3 Determine end of an interval by going to **Media | Playback | Stop** or key command [**F8**].

After each pause with [**F7**] or corresponding command the playhead rewinds corresponding to **File → Options**, the **Audio/Video** tab and the setting made at *Skip back on play in transcribe mode*.

The result is a transcript row corresponding to the interval from the first Start to End of interval but no selection along the timeline.

If instead [**F11**] and [**F12**] are used during Play Mode Transcribe then a transcript row is created and a selection along the timeline is made. Start and stop must however be made with [**F7**] and [**F8**].

Merging Transcript Rows

Sometimes there is a need of cleaning up or reduce the number of transcript rows. Merging rows can be a handy solution.

♦ **Follow These Steps**

1 Open a media item in edit mode.

2 Select two or more transcript rows by holding down the [**Ctrl**] key and left-clicking in the item number column of the transcript rows.

3 Go to **Layout | Rows & Columns | Merge Rows**.

The merged row now covers the timespan from the first to the last selected timeslots.

Importing Transcripts

Frequently, when the transcripts are separate documents there is a need to import the material into given place within a project. The style formats that will be accepted for such import are Timestamp, Paragraph, and Table. The file formats need to be .DOC, .DOCX, .RTF, or .TXT.

The *Timestamp* Style format:

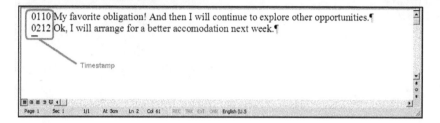

The *Paragraph* Style format:

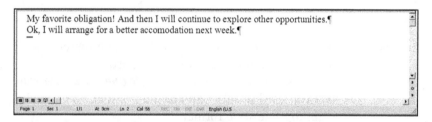

The *Table* Style format:

Timespan¤	Content¤	Speaker¤	¤	
0110¤	My favorite obligation! And then I will continue to explore other opportunities.¤	Ruth¤	¤	
0212¤	Ok, I will arrange for a better accomodation next week.¤	Edgar¤	¤	
¶				

Page 1   Sec 1   1/1   At 4,5cm   Ln 5   Col 6   REC   TRK   EXT   OVR   English (U.S

To import a transcript file:

♦ **Follow These Steps**
  1 Open the media item.
  2 Go to **External Data | Import | Rows**.

The **Import Transcript Entries** dialog box now appears:

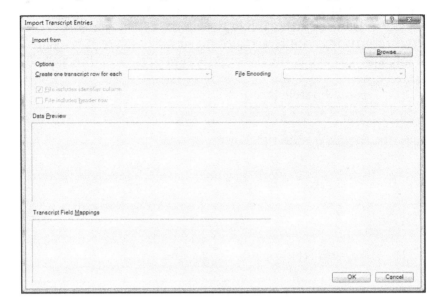

3   The [**Browse...**] button gives access to a file browser and you can select the file you want tio import.

4   Once a file is selected at *Options, Create one transcript row for each* you need to select an alternative that corresponds to the appropriate style format.

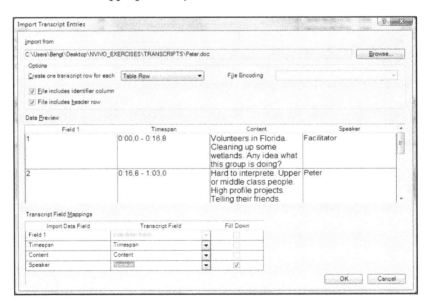

5   When Data Preview displays a correct image of the transcript then you need to set the Transcript Field

Mappings so that imported data are mapped to the proper columns in the media item.

6 Confirm with [**OK**].

Note, that when more columns are included in the imported file these columns are also created in NVivo:

Timespan	Content	Speaker
1	0:00,0 - 0:16,8	Volunteers in Florida. Cleaning up some wetlands. Any idea what this group is doing?	Facilitator
2	0:16,8 - 1:03,0	Hard to interprete. Upper or middle class people. High profile projects. Telling their friends.	Peter
3	1:03,0 - 1:23,5	Con is working with teenagers on a Youth center. Helping them with career choises.	Facilitator
4	1:23,5 - 2:03,0	Working with problematic teenagers is not very fun, but he thinks he can make a contribution to his society.	Peter

Transcript rows can also be hidden:

♦ **Follow These Steps**

1 Go to **Media | Display | Transcript → Hide**.

This is a toggling function.

You may also hide/unhide the video player in a video item:

♦ **Follow These Steps**

1 Go to **Media | Display | Video Player**.

This is a toggling function.

For video items you may also want to display the transcript rows below the media timeline and the video player:

♦ **Follow These Steps**

1 Open a video item.

2 Go to **Media | Display | Transcript → Bottom**.

Coding a Media Item

Coding a media item can be made in two dimensions of the material:

1. The transcript row or words in the transcript.
2. A timeslot along the timeline.

The coding principles are the same for media items as for any text material. Select a text or an interval that shall be coded and then select the node or nodes that the selection to be coded. If you want to code a whole transcript row, select the row by clicking the item number column, then right-click and select the node or nodes that you want to code at.

If you want to code a certain timeslot along the timeline, make a selection and then select the node or nodes (see Chapter 9, Introducing Nodes and Chapter 13, About Coding).

	Timespan	Content	Speaker
2	0:16,8 - 1:03,0	Hard to interprete. Upper or middle class people. High profile projects. Telling their friends.	Peter
3	1:03,0 - 1:23,5	Con is working with teenagers on a Youth center. Helping them with career choises.	Facilitator
4	1:23,5 - 2:03,0	Working with problematic teenagers is not very fun, but he thinks he can make a contribution to his society.	Peter
5	2:03,0 - 2:10,5	What's his motivation?	Facilitator

Shadow Coding

Shadow Coding is a special feature related to coding of audio items. It means that when a text or a row in a transcript has been coded the corresponding interval of the timeline has been shadow coded and vice versa. Shadow coding can only be shown as coding stripes (see page 166). Coding stripes are filled colored lines and shadow coding stripes are lighter colored stripes (both of same color). The audio item above is coded at the nodes Management and Public Service. Both the transcript row and the timeslot are coded at the node Management. Therefore the item has 'double' coding stripes. The node Public Service is only coded at the transcript row. Shadow coding has no use other than being a graphic help when studying coding stripes. Shadow coding can be switched off with **View** | **Coding** | **Shadow Coding**, which is a toggling function.

Sometimes there is a need of selecting a timespan from an existing transcript.

♦ **Follow These Steps**
  1 Open a media item with transcript rows.
  2 Select a transcript row.
  3 Go to **Media** | **Select** | **Select Media from Transcript**.

Now there is an exact selection and you can play, code or link from this selection.

The following method is a practical way to play an interval from a transcript row:

♦ **Follow These Steps**
  1 Open a media item with transcript rows.
  2 Select a transcript row.
  3 Go to **Media** | **Selection** | **Play Transcript Media**.

Only the selected interval will played.

If you want to open a node then click on a coding stripe, open the **Audio** tab and now you can see both the timeline and the transcript row. Playing from here only plays the coded timeslot(s).

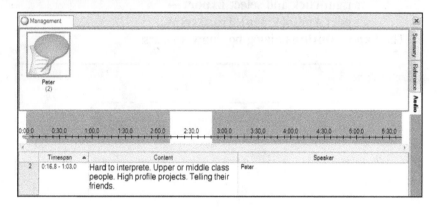

About autocoding of transcripts, see page 159.

Linking from a Media Item

An audio item can be linked (Memo Links, See Also Links and Annotations) in the same manner as any other NVivo item. However, hyperlinks cannot be created from an audio item. Links can be created from a selected timespan or from the transcript.

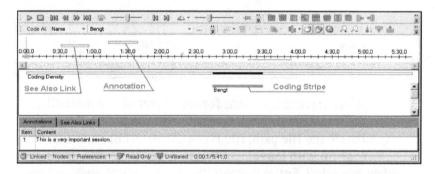

A Memo Link is shown in the list view. A See Also Link or an Annotation that refers to a timespan are shown above the timeline as a filled pink line and a filled blue line respectively. Coding stripes are shown below the timeline (see also Chapter 8, Memos, Links, and Annotations).

Exporting a Media Item

♦ **Follow These Steps**
 1 Click [**Sources**] in area (**1**).
 2 Select the **Internals** folder in area (**2**) or its subfolder.
 3 Select the media item or items in area (**3**) that you want to export.

4   Go to **External Data | Export | Export →
     Export Audio(Video)/Transcript...**
     or key command **[Ctrl]** + **[Shift]** + **[E]**
     or right-click and select **Export →
     Export Audio(Video)/Transcript...**
The **Export Options** dialog box now appears:

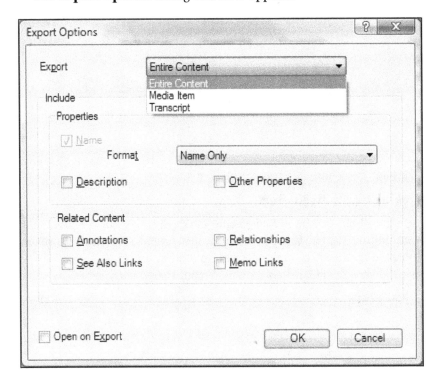

5   Select applicable options for the export of the mediafile,
     the transcript or both. Confirm with **[OK]**.
6   Decide the file path, file type (*.HTM, *.HTML) and filename,
     confirm with **[Save]**.
When you select *Entire Content* the result is a web page and the
media file and other supporting files are stored in a folder called
"Filename_files". If you also select the option *Open on Export* then
the web browser opens and the result is shown instantly.

- ♦ -

A media item can also be printed with the normal command **File
→ Print → Print** or key command **[Ctrl]** + **[P]**. A transcript and its
coding stripes can similarly be printed.

Deleting a Media Item

♦ **Follow These Steps**

1   Click [**Sources**] in area (**1**).
2   Select the **Internals** folder in area (**2**) or its subfolder.
3   Select the media item or items in area (**3**) that you want to delete.
4   Use the [**Del**] key
    or go to **Home** | **Editing** | **Delete**
    or right-click and select **Delete**.
5   Confirm with [**Yes**].

7. HANDLING PICTURE-SOURCES

NVivo 9 can import the following picture formats: .BMP, .GIF, .JPG, .JPEG, .TIF and .TIFF.

Importing Picture Files

♦ **Follow These Steps**

   1   Go to **External Data | Import | Import Pictures**.
       Default folder is **Internals.**
       Go to 5.

alternatively

   1   Click [**Sources**] in area (**1**).
   2   Select the **Internals** folder in area (**2**) or its subfolder.
   3   Go to **External Data | Import | Import Pictures**
       or key command [**Ctrl**] + [**Shift**] + [**I**].
       Go to 5.

alternatively

   3   Click on any empty space in area (**3**).
   4   Right-click and select **Import Internals → Import Pictures...**

The **Import Internals** dialog box now appears:

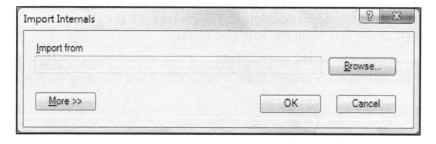

   5   The [**Browse...**] button gives access to a filebrowser and you can select one or several picture files for a batch import.
   6   When the picture files have been selected, confirm with [**Open**].
   7   Finally, when desired options have been chosen the import takes place with [**OK**].

When only *one* picture file has been imported the **Picture Properties** dialog box appears:

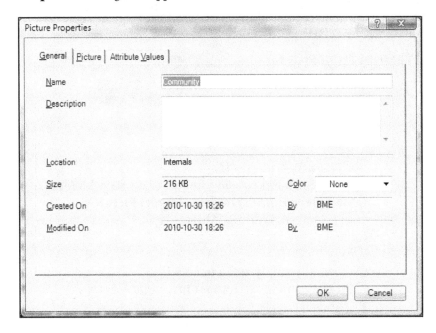

This dialog box makes it possible to modify the name of the item and optionally add a description. The **Picture** tab gives access to details and data from the imported picture:

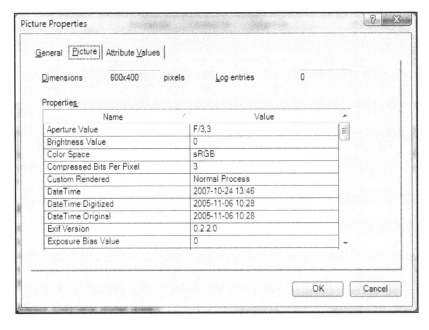

7   Confirm with [**OK**].

Here is a typical list view in area **(3)** of some picture items:

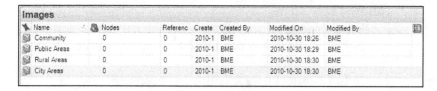

Opening a Picture Item

♦ **Follow These Steps**
  1 Click [**Sources**] in area **(1)**.
  2 Select the **Internals** folder in area **(2)** or its subfolder.
  3 Select the picture item in area **(3)** that you want to open.
  4 Go to **Home | Item | Open**
     or key command [**Ctrl**] + [**Shift**] + [**O**]
     or right-click and select **Open Picture...**
     or double-click the picture item in area **(3)**.
An open picture item can look like this:

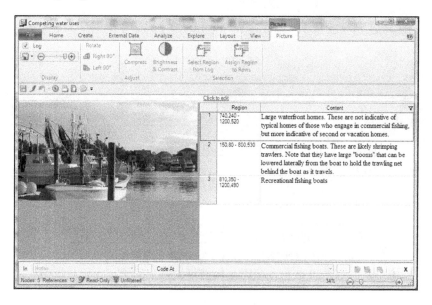

The handling of pictures is about defining a *Region* of the picture which then can be associated with a written note, a *Picture Log.* Both a Region and a Picture Log can be coded and linked.

Selecting a Region and Creating a Picture Log

◆ **Follow These Steps**

1   Select a corner of the Region with the left mouse button, then drag the mouse pointer to the opposite corner and release the button.

2   Go to **Layout | Rows & Columns | Insert → Row**
or key command **[Ctrl] + [Ins]**.

The result can appear like this and the Picture Log can be typed in the cell below the column head *Content*.

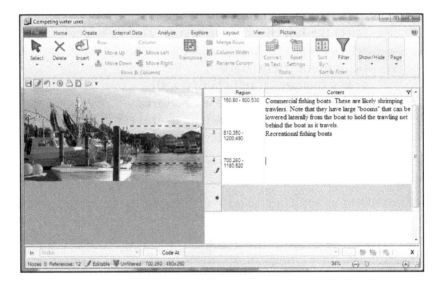

Sometimes you may need to redefine a Region and a Picture Log.

◆ **Follow These Steps**

1   Select the row of the Picture Log that you wish to redefine. When selecting a Row the corresponding Region is highlighted.

2   Select a new Region (redefine a highlighted area).

3   Go to **Picture | Selection | Assign Region to Rows**.

In this way you adjust both a Region and a Row of the Picture Log.

As an alternative you can use a Row from which you can select a new Region.

◆ **Follow These Steps**

1   Select a Row of the Picture Log. Corresponding region will be highlighted.

2   Go to **Picture | Selection | Select Region from Log**.

You can also hide the Picture Log:

◆ **Follow These Steps**

1   Go to **Picture | Display | Log**.

This is a toggling function and a Picture item with a hidden Picture Log appears like this:

Editing Pictures

NVivo 9 offers some basic functions for easy editing of picture items. The following functions are menu options after a picture item has been opened:

Picture | Adjust | Rotate → Right 90°
Picture | Adjust | Rotate → Left 90°
Picture | Adjust | Compress
Picture | Adjust | Brightness & Contrast

Coding a Picture Item

You can code a Picture Log, a selected text element or a Region of a picture item. The act of coding is in principle the same way you would code other elements of your NVivo project. In short you select data to be coded and then you select the node or nodes that the data will be coded at (see Chapter 9, Introducing Nodes and Chapter 13, About Coding).

If you need to code a row of the picture log, select the row by clicking the leftmost column of the row, right-clicking and selecting a node or nodes.

If instead (or in addition) you need to code a Region, select the Region and select a node or nodes as usual.

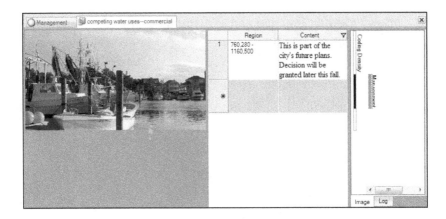

Coding stripes for a picture item are always shown in a window to the left and in a position leveled with the region. Coding stripes from a coded region are colored and filled while coding stripes from a coded picture log are lighter colored. (Same look as Shadow coding stripes.) The above example shows a picture item that has been coded at the node The Star. Both the region and the picture log have been directly coded and therefore "double" coding stripes are shown.

Sometimes there is a need of selecting a Region outgoing from a Row of the Picture Log.

♦ **Follow These Steps**
1 Open a picture item.
2 Select a row of the Picture Log.
3 Go to **Picture → Select Region from Log**.

The result can be used to code on, or create links as required:

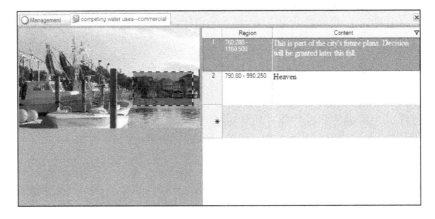

We would also like to show when the *node* Management has been opened. After having clicked the Picture tab to the right you will see both the coded region of the picture and the corresponding Picture Log.

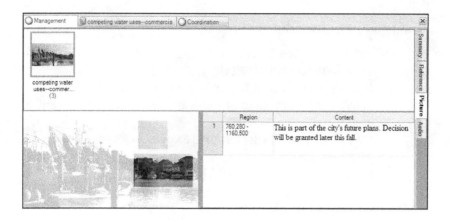

Linking from a Picture Item

A picture item can be linked (Memo Links, See Also Links and Annotations) in the same manner as any other NVivo item. However, hyperlinks cannot be created from a picture item. Links can be created from a selected region or from the Picture log. A Memo Link is not shown elsewhere than in the list view. See Also Linka or Annotations are shown as pink and blue frames respectively:

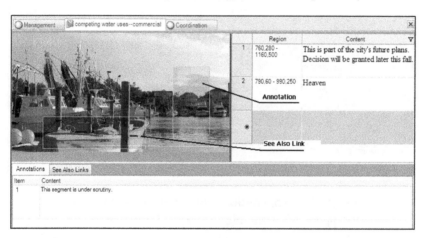

See also Chapter 8, Memos, Links, and Annotations.

Exporting a Picture Item

◆ **Follow These Steps**

1 Click [**Sources**] in area (**1**).
2 Select the **Internals** folder in area (**2**) or its subfolder.
3 Select the picture item or items in area (**3**) that you want to export.
4 Go to **External Data | Export | Export → Export Picture/Log**
  or key command [**Ctrl**] + [**Shift**] + [**E**]
  or right-click and select **Export → Picture/Log...**

The **Export Options** dialog box now appears:

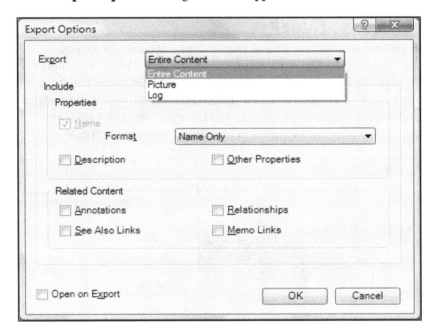

5 Select applicable options, which allows for the export of . the picture file, the picture log or both. Confirm with [**OK**].
6 Decide file name, file location, and file type, confirm with [**Save**].

When you select *Entire Content* the result is a web page with the picture file in a folder called "Filename_files". Your web browser will open and the result is instantly shown if you also check the option *Open on Export.*

- ◆ -

A picture item can also be printed with the normal command **File → Print → Print** or key command [**Ctrl**] + [**P**]. The picture, the transcript and the coding stripes can be printed.

Deleting a Picture Item

♦ **Follow These Steps**

1 Click [**Sources**] in area (**1**).
2 Select the **Internals** folder in area (**2**) or its subfolder.
3 Select the picture item or items in area (**3**) that you want to delete.
4 Use the [**Del**] key
 or Go to **Home | Editing | Delete**
 or right-click and select **Delete**.
5 Confirm with [**Yes**].

8. MEMOS, LINKS, AND ANNOTATIONS

Exploring Links in the List View

Memo Links, See Also Links, and Annotations (but not Hyperlinks) can be displayed in List View in area (3) like any other project item.

♦ **Follow These Steps**
1 Click [**Folders**] in area (1).
2 Select any of the following folders in area (2):
Memo Links
See Also Links
Annotations

Then you will see the selected list of links as items in area (3).

Selecting a **Memo Link** item in area (3) and right-clicking will open a menu with the options: Open Linked Item, Open Linked Memo or Delete Memo Link. Exporting and printing the whole list of items are also available options.

Double-clicking a **See Also Link** in area (3) opens the **See Also Link Properties** dialog box. Right-clicking on such item will open a menu with the options: Open From Item, Open To Item, Edit See Also Link or Delete See Also Link. Exporting and printing the whole list of items are also available options.

Double-clicking an **Annotation** item in area (3) opens the source and its Annotation in area (4). Right-clicking on such item will open a menu with the options: Open Source and Delete Annotation. Exporting and printing the whole list of items are also available options.

Memos

Memos are shorter notes or instructions akin to Post-it notes. For example memos can be field notes that have been created outside NVivo. A memo link can only be applied to one project item, and each project item can only be linked to one memo. A memo cannot be linked to another memo with a Memo Link.

As with other project items you can import them or create them with NVivo. The following file formats can be imported as memos: .DOC, .DOCX, .RTF, .TXT, and .PDF.

Importing a Memo

♦ **Follow These Steps**

1 Go to **External Data | Import | Memos**.
Default folder is **Memos**.
Go to 5.

alternatively

1 Click [**Sources**] in area (**1**).
2 Select the **Memos** folder in area (**2**) or its subfolder.
3 Go to **External Data | Import | Memos**
or key command [**Ctrl**] + [**Shift**] + [**I**].
Go to 5.

alternatively

3 Click on any empty space in area (**3**).
4 Right-click and select **Import Memos...**

The **Import Memos** dialog box now appears:

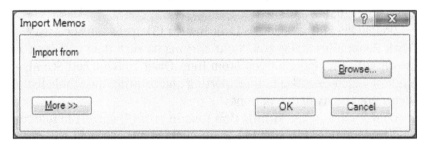

5 The [**Browse...**] button gives access to a filebrowser and you can select one or several documents for a batch import.
6 When the documents have been selected, confirm with [**Open**].

The [**More** >>] button gives acces to several options:

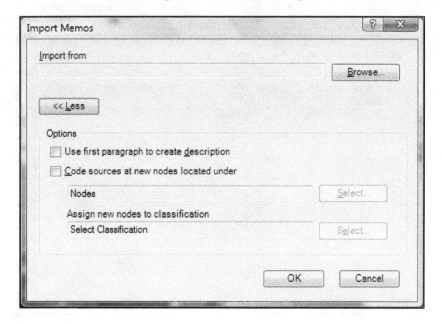

Use first paragraph to create description: NVivo copies the first paragraph of the document and pastes it into the description text box.

Code sources at new nodes located under: Each source item will be coded at a node with the same name as the imported file and located under the folder and parent node that has been selected. Also you must assign the nodes to a Classification when importing. See page 130 about Classification Sheets.

  7   Confirm the import with [**OK**].

Creating a Memo

◆ **Follow These Steps**
  1   Go to **Create | Sources | Memo**.
      Default folder is **Memos**.
      Go to 5.

alternatively
  1   Click [**Sources**] in area (**1**).
  2   Select the **Memos** folder in area (**2**) or its subfolder.
  3   Go to **Create | Sources | Memo**
      or key command [**Ctrl**] + [**Shift**] + [**N**].
      Go to 5.

alternatively
  3   Click on any empty space in area (**3**).
  4   Right-click and select **New Memo...**

The **New Memo** dialog box now appears:

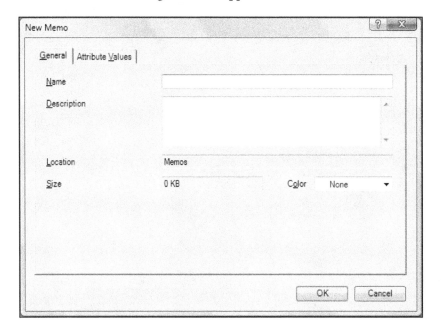

5　Type a name (compulsory) and a description (optional), then [**OK**].

Here is a typical list view in area (**3**) of some memos:

Opening a Memo

♦　**Follow These Steps**

1　Click [**Sources**] in area (**1**).

2　Select the **Memos** folder in area (**2**) or its subfolder.

3　Select a memo in area (**3**) that you want to open.

4　Go to **Home | Item | Open**
or key command [**Ctrl**] + [**Shift**] + [**O**]
or right-click and select **Open Memo...**
or double-click on the memo in area (**3**).

Please note, you can only open one memo at a time, but several memos can stay open.

Creating a Memo Link

♦ **Follow These Steps**

1 In the list view, area **(3),** select the item from which you want to create a Memo Link. You cannot create a Memo Link to a memo that is already linked.

2 Go to **Analyze | Links → Memo Link → Link to Existing Memo...**

or right-click and select **Memo Link → Link to Existing Memo...**

The **Select Project Item** dialog box now appears. Only unlinked memos can be selected, linked memos are dimmed.

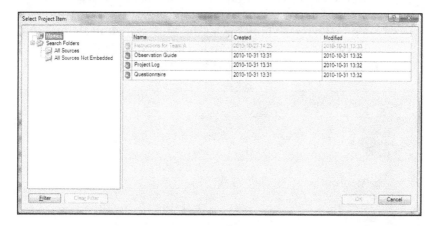

3 Select the memo that you want to link to and confiorm with **[OK]**.

The Memo Link is shown in the list view in area **(3)** with one icon for the memo and one icon for the linked item.

Creating a Memo Link and a New Memo Simultaneously

♦ **Follow These Steps**

1 In the list view, area **(3),** select the item from which you want to create a Memo Link and a new Memo.

2 Go to **Analyze | Links → Memo Link → Link to New Memo...**

or key command **[Ctrl] + [Shift] + [K]**

or right-click and select **Memo Link → Link to New Memo...**

The **New Memo** dialog box appears and you continue according to page 106.

Opening a Linked Memo

♦ **Follow These Steps**

1   In the list view, area (**3**), select the item from which you want to open a Linked Memo.

2   Go to **Analyze | Links → Memo Link → Open Linked Memo**
or key command [**Ctrl**] + [**Shift**] + [**M**]
or right-click and select **Memo Link → Open Linked Memo**.

Deleting a Memo Link

♦ **Follow These Steps**

1   In the list view, area (**3**), select the item from which you want to delete a Memo Link.

2   Go to **Analyze | Links → Memo Link → Delete Memo Link**
or right-click and select **Memo Link → Delete Memo Link**.

The **Delete Confirmation** dialog box now appears:

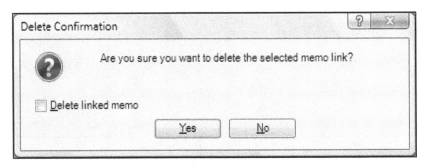

3   If you select *Delete linked memo* then also the Memo will be deleted, otherwise only the Memo Link will be deleted. Confirm with [**Yes**].

Deleting a Memo

♦ **Follow These Steps**

1   Click [**Sources**] in area (**1**).

2   Select the **Memos** folder in area (**2**) or its subfolder.

3   Select the memo or memos in area (**3**) that you want to delete.

4   Go to **Home | Editing | Delete**
or use the [**Del**] key
or right-click and select **Delete**.

5   Confirm with [**Yes**].

See Also Links

See Also Links are links from a selection (text, picture) in an item to another item or a certain selection of another item. Unlike Memo Links, See Also Links allow multiple selections to be linked to the same target.

Creating a See Also Link to Another Item

♦ **Follow These Steps**

1 Open the item from which you want to create a See Also Link.

2 Select the section (text, picture) from which you want to create a See Also Link.

3 Go to **Analyze | Links → See Also Link → New See Also Link...**

or right-click and select **Links → See Also Link → New See Also Link...**

The **New See Also Link** dialog box now appears:

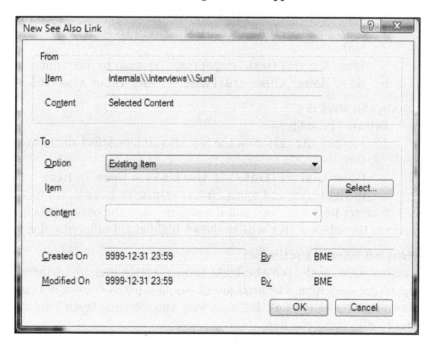

Under **Option**, you can select what type of project item you will link. If you select an option starting with *New* then an item will be created. If you select the option *Existing Item* you go to the [**Select...**] button and use the **Select Project Item** dialog box to select an item to link to. When the item has been selected the link goes to the entire target item. Confirm with [**OK**].

For example, in this source document the See Also Link is indicated as a pink colored highlighting:

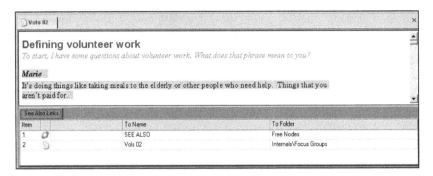

Creating a See Also Link to a Selection of Another Item

♦ **Follow These Steps**

1 Open the target item that you want to link to.
2 Select the section (text, image) that you want to link to.
3 Copy with for example [**Ctrl**] + [**C**].
4 Open the item from which you want to create a See Also Link.
5 Select the area (text, image) that you want to link from.
6 Go to **Home | Clipboard | Paste → Paste As See Also Link**.

Opening a See Also Link

♦ **Follow These Steps**

1 Position the cursor on the See Also Link or select the entire link.
2 Go to **Analyze | Links | Se Also Links → Open To Item** or right-click and select **Links → Open To Item**.

The target item will open and if you have used the option *Selected Content* the selected area will be shown highlighted otherwise not.

Hiding or Unhiding See Also Links

You can view all the See Also Links from a certain item in a window below the open item. The links are shown as a list of items. Clicking on an item opens the link. Right-clicking and selecting **Open To Item...** also opens the link.

♦ **Follow These Steps**

1 Open the item that has one or several See Also Links.
2 Go to **View | Links | See Also Links**.

This is a toggling function for hiding or unhiding the See Also Link window.

Opening a Linked External Source

Provided the See Also Link leads to an external item, you are able to open that external source (file or web site) directly. You may wish to create links to external sources rather than creating hyperlinks as you may reduce unnecessary modifications to the external sources.

♦ **Follow These Steps**

   1   Position the cursor on the See Also Link or select the entire link.

   2   Go to **Analyze | Links | See Also Links → Open Linked External File**
or right-click and select **Links → Open Linked External File**.

Deleting a See Also Link

♦ **Follow These Steps**

   1   Position the cursor on the See Also Link or select the entire link.

   2   Go to **Analyze | Links | See Also Link → Delete See Also Link**
or right-click and select **Links → See Also Link → Delete See Also Link**.

   3   Confirm with [**Yes**].

Annotations

An annotation in NVivo shares similarities with a footnote in Word. The Annotations, however, behave more like a link from a certain text section (or image) area to a separate textbox. Annotations are numbered within each project item.

Creating an Annotation

♦ **Follow These Steps**

   1   Open a source item or a node.

   2   Select the text or other section area that you want to link to an Annotation.

   3   Go to **Analyze | Annotation → New Annotation...**
or right-click and select **Links → Annotation → New Annotation**.

A new window will open where the annotation can be typed. The linked area is then shown highlighted in blue.

Does it fit with your goals? Do you expect to have enough time to do what you want to do?
Yes that's really the goal. Spare time is a dream.

Annotations	
Item	Content
1	
2	

Hiding or Unhiding Annotations

♦ **Follow These Steps**

1 Open the project item that contains Annotations.

2 Go to **View | Links | Annotations**.

This is a toggling function and is valid separately for each item.

Deleting an Annotation

♦ **Follow These Steps**

1 Position the cursor on the link to an Annotation.

2 Go to **Analyze | Annotation | Delete Annotation** or right-click and select **Links → Annotation → Delete Annotation**.

3 Confirm with [**Yes**].

Hyperlinks

NVivo can create links to external sources in two ways:

- Hyperlinks from a source item.
- External items (see page 60).

Creating Hyperlinks

♦ **Follow These Steps**

1 Select a section (text or image) in a source item while in Edit mode.

2 Go to **Analyze | Links | Hyperlink → New Hyperlink...** or right-click and select **Links → Hyperlink → New Hyperlink...**

The **New Hyperlink** dialog box now appears:

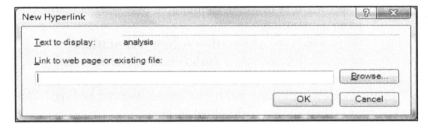

3 Paste a complete URL or use [**Browse...**] to find the target file in your computer or in your local network.

4 Confirm with [**OK**].

The Hyperlink will be blue and underlined.

Opening a Hyperlink

The following three methods will open a Hyperlink:

♦ **Follow These Steps**

1 Position the cursor on the link.

2 Go to **Analyze | Links | Hyperlink → Open Hyperlink**.

alternatively

♦ **Follow These Steps**

1 Point at the link with the mouse poiner which will then become an arrow.

2 Right-click and select **Links → Hyperlink → Open Hyperlink**.

alternatively

♦ **Follow These Steps**

1 Hold down the **[Ctrl]** key.

2 Click on the link.

This latter command will sometimes cause the external file (depending on the file type) to open as a minimized window. If this is the case then you can either repeat this command or click on the program button of the Windows toolbar so the window opens fully.

9. INTRODUCING NODES

A Node is, broadly, a category. Nodes can mean concepts, processes, thoughts, ideas, products, geographical places and even people. Nodes become increasingly important as a study develops and its concepts and theories mature. Data contained in a node can be anything from a single letter to a complete document.

Some researchers know very early on in their project what kind of nodes they will need to organize and categorize their data. They can create nodes before they start to work with their source material. Other researchers may need to brainstorm organizational categories, concepts and structures 'on the fly' as they work through their source material. The way you work with nodes varies largely depending on the methods used, the research situation and your personality.

Early on in any project, a good idea is to identify a few nodes that you think will be useful. These early nodes can be coded at as you work through your data for the first time. These early nodes can be moved, merged, renamed, redefined or even deleted later on as your project develops.

NVivo has developed a system for organizing and classifying both source items and nodes (see Chapter 10, About Classifications).

The terms *Parent Node*, *Child Node* and *Aggregate* are used when NVivo's node system is described.

A *Parent Node* is the next higher hierarchical node in relation to its *Child Nodes.*

Aggregate means that a certain Node in any hierarchical level accomodates the logical sum of all its nearest Child Nodes. Each node can at any point of time activate or deactivate the function Aggregate and with immediate effect. The Aggregate control is in the **New Node** dialog box or **Node Properties** dialog box.

Creating a Node

♦   **Follow These Steps**
1   Go to **Create** | **Nodes** | **Node**.
    Default folder is **Nodes**.
    Go to 5.
    alternatively
1   Click [**Nodes**] in are **(1)**.
2   Select the **Nodes** folder in area **(2)** or its subfolder.
3   Go to **Create** | **Nodes** | **Node**
    or key command [**Ctrl**] + [**Shift**] + [**N**]
    Go to 5.
    alternatively

3 Click on any empty space in area (**3**).
4 Right-click and select **New Node...**
The **New Node** dialog box now appears:

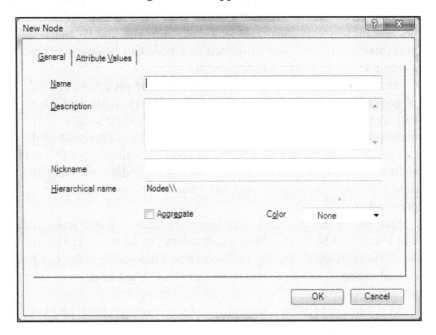

5 Type name (compulsory) and a description and a nickname (both optional), then [**OK**].

Here is a typical list view in area (**3**) of some nodes:

Deleting a Node

◆ **Follow These Steps**
1 Click [**Nodes**] in area (**1**).
2 Select the **Nodes** folder in area (**2**) or its subfolder.
3 Select the node or nodes in area (**3**) that you want to delete.
4 Go to **Home | Editing | Delete**
   or use the [**Del**] key
   or go to **Edit → Delete**
   or right-click and select **Delete**.
5 Confirm with [**Yes**].

Building Hierarchical Nodes

Nodes can be organized hierarchically. As such there are node headings and subheadings in several levels. Nodes can therefore form a sort of structured terminology, such as the MeSH (Medical Subject Headings) used by the MEDLINE/PubMed article database.

Creating a Child Node

♦   **Follow These Steps**
1   Click **[Nodes]** in area **(1)**.
2   Select the **Nodes** folder in area **(2)** or its subfolder.
3   Select the node to which you want to create a Child Node.
4   Go to **Create | Nodes | Node**
     or key command **[Ctrl] + [Shift] + [N]**
     or right-click and select **New Node...**
The **New Node** dialog box now appears.
5   Type a name (compulsory) and a description and a nickname (both optional), then **[OK]**.

It is also possible to move the tree nodes within the list view, area **(3)**, with drag-and-drop or cut and paste.

Here is a typical list view in area **(3)** of some hierarchical nodes:

Tree Nodes			
Name	Sources	References	Created On
Topics - Interviews	0	0	2006-02-16 03:46
Topics - Focus Groups	0	0	2006-02-16 03:46
time	0	0	2006-02-16 03:38
Name	**Sources**	**References**	**Created On**
time as money	5	5	2006-02-16 03:38
taking time	2	3	2006-02-16 03:38
'spare' time	5	8	2006-02-16 03:38

Underlying items in the list can be opened or closed by clicking the + or − symbols, but also by using **View | List View | List View→ Expand All (Selected) Nodes/ Collapse All (Selected) Nodes**. A useful function is showing Child Node Headers. When these headers are displayed you can modify the column widths. Apply **View | List View | List View → Child Node Headers** (toggling).

Deleting a Parent Node

When you delete any Parent Node you also delete all its Child Nodes.

♦   **Follow These Steps**
1   Click **[Nodes]** in area **(1)**.
2   Select the **Nodes** folder in area **(2)** or its subfolder.
3   Select the node or nodes in area **(3)** that you want to delete.
4   Go to **Home | Editing | Delete**
     or use the **[Del]** key
     or right-click and select **Delete**.
5   Confirm with **[Yes]**.

Relationships

Relationships are nodes that indicate that two project items (source items or nodes) are related such as the hypothesis *Poverty* influences *Public Health*. Data supporting that hypothesis could be coded at such relationship node.

Different relationship types are defined by the user and are stored under [**Classifications**] and the **Relationship Types** folder. The relationship nodes are then created as associative, one way, or symmetrical.

The folder Relationships is not allowed to have subfolders and these nodes can not be arranged hierarchically. Classifications cannot be assigned to Relationships.

Creating a Relationship Type

Before creating relationships amongst your data, you must create some relationship types.

♦   **Follow These Steps**
    1   Go to **Create | Classifications | Relationship Type**
        Default folder is **Relationship Types**.
        Go to 5.
alternatively
    1   Click [**Classifications**] in area **(1)**.
    2   Select the **Relationship Types** folder in area **(2)**.
    3   Go to **Create | Classifications | Relationship Type**
        or key command [**Ctrl**] + [**Shift**] + [**N**].
        Go to 5.
alternatively
    3   Click on any empty space in area **(3)**.
    4   Right-click and select **New Relationship Type...**
The **New Relationship Type** dialog box now appears:

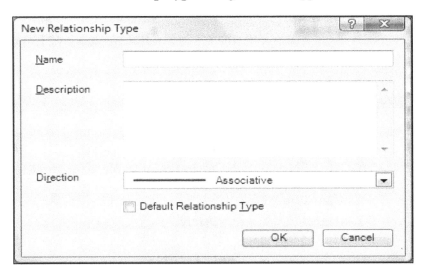

5 Select *Associative, One Way* or *Symmetrical* from the drop-down list at **Direction**.

6 Type a name (compulsory) and a description (optional), then [**OK**].

The list view with Relationship Types in area (**3**), may look like this:

	Default	Name	Direction	Created On	Modified On	Created By
	✓	Associated	——	2006-02-16 01:01	2006-02-16 01:01	KMC
		dec[Name]	——→	2006-02-22 23:53	2006-02-22 23:53	KMC
		impacts	——→	2006-02-16 04:01	2006-02-16 04:01	KMC
		is friends with	——→	2006-02-16 04:01	2006-02-16 04:01	KMC
		lives with	——	2006-02-16 04:01	2006-02-22 04:02	KMC

Deleting a Relationship Type

◆ **Follow These Steps**

1 Click [**Classifications**] in area (**1**).

2 Select the **Relationship Types** folder in area (**2**).

3 Select the Relationship Type or Types in area (**3**) that you want to delete.

4 Go to **Home** | **Editing** | **Delete**
or use the [**Del**] key
or right-click and select **Delete**.

5 Confirm with [**Yes**].

Creating a Relationship

◆ **Follow These Steps**

1 Go to **Create** | **Nodes** | **Relationships**.
Default folder is **Relationships**.
Go to 5.

alternatively

1 Click [**Nodes**] in area (**1**).

2 Select the **Relationships** folder in area (**2**).

3 Go to **Create** | **Nodes** | **Relationships**
or key command [**Ctrl**] + [**Shift**] + [**N**].
Go to 5.

alternatively

3 Click on any empty space in area (**3**).

4 Right-click and select **New Relationship...**

The **New Relationship** dialog box now appears:

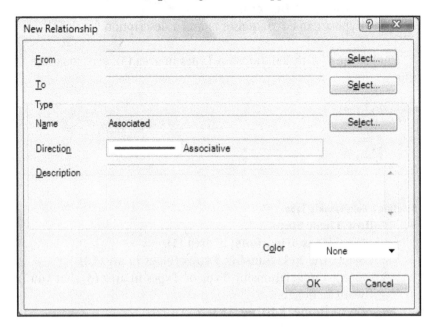

A Relationship defines a relation between two project items: source items or nodes.

> 5   Use the [**Select...**] buttons to find the items that will be connected by this node.

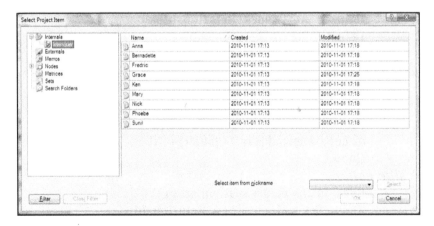

> 6   Select one From-item and one To-item. Confirm with [**OK**].
>
> 7   Select a Relationship Type with [**Select...**] under **Type**.

The dialog box will then look like this:

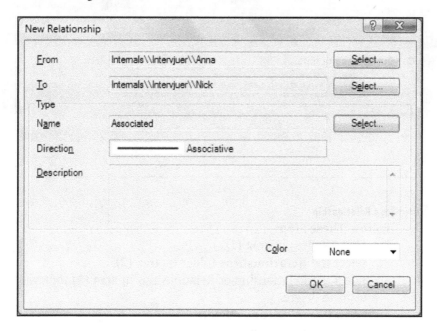

New Relationship

From	Internals\\Intervjuer\\Anna	Select...
To	Internals\\Intervjuer\\Nick	Select...

Type

Name	Associated	Select...
Direction	——————— Associative	
Description		

Color   None

OK   Cancel

8   Confirm with [**OK**].
The list view with Relationships in area (**3**), may look like this:

Relationships

From Na	From Folder	Type	To Name	To Folder	Direction	Source	Referenc	Created	Modified
Anna	Cases	lives with	Sunil	Cases	——————	0	0	2006-02-	2006-02-
Bernadette	Cases	is friends wit	Ken	Cases	————▶	0	0	2006-02-	2006-02-
Ken	Cases	is friends wit	Bernadette	Cases	————▶	0	0	2006-02-	2006-02-
time\lack o	Tree Nodes	decreases	Motivation	Free Nodes	————▶	3	8	2006-02-	2006-02-
Annette	Cases	Associated	personal goa	Tree Nodes	——————	0	0	2007-01-	2007-01-

View a Relationship from a Related Item

◆   **Follow These Steps**

1   Open an item in area (**3**) that has a relationship.
2   Go to **View | Links → Relationships**
which is a toggling function.

A new window will open and the relationship will show.

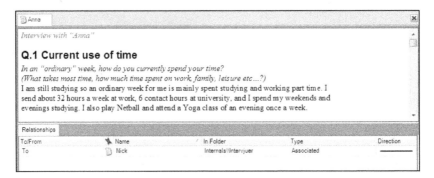

Deleting a Relationship

♦ **Follow These Steps**

1 Click [**Nodes**] in area (**1**).

2 Select the **Relationships** folder in area (**2**).

3 Select the Relationship or Relationships in area (**3**) that you want to delete.

4 Go to **Home | Editing | Delete**
or use the [**Del**] **key**
or right-click and select **Delete**.

5 Confirm with [**Yes**].

10. ABOUT CLASSIFICATIONS

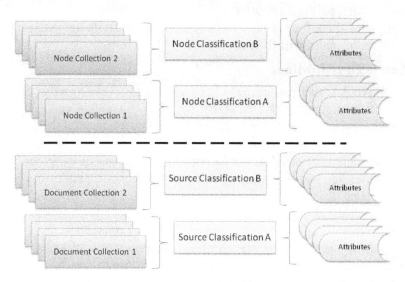

Node and Source Classifications

Nodes, Classifications and Attributes are related in the following way.

Source Items hold primary or secondary data. They can be document items, media items or picture items.

Nodes represent a topic, a phenomenon, an idea, a value, an opinion, or any other abstraction or tangible object thought to be important for the current study.

Attributes represent characteristics or properties of a source item or a node which has or will have an impact when analyzing data. Each such attribute has a set of *Values*.

Classifications are defined by NVivo as a collective name for a certain set of Attributes that will be assigned to certain source items or nodes.

Node Classifications

An example: A study is about pupils, teachers, politicians and schools. There are reasons to create individual nodes for eah of these four groups. Attributes for pupils could then be: Age, gender, grade, number of siblings, social class.

Attributes for teachers could then be: Age, gender, education, number of years as teacher, school subject.

Attributes for politicians could then be: Age, gender, political preference, number of years as politician, other profile.

Attributes for schools could then be: Size, age, size of the community, political majority.

Each of these four groups needs its own set of attributes. Each such set of nodes will then form a Node Classification.

Source Classifications

In NVivo 9, Classifications have been applied to source items with attributes and values. Source Classifications, for example, could be applied to certain interviews that may need attributes like the time of the inteview for longitudinal studies, place and other conditions. Source Classifications can also be applied to literature reviews with attributes like journal name, type of study, keywords, publication date, name of authors etc.

Classifications therefore fall into two types: Node Classifications and Source Classifications. We will explore how to create Classifications, how they are associated with source items and nodes and how individual values are handled. Attributes cannot be created without the existence of Classifications. This chapter presents examples of how to create a Node Classification, but the procedures are similar for Source Classifications.

Creating a Classification

♦ **Follow These Steps**

1   Go to **Create | Classifications | Node Classification**
     Default folder is **Node Classifications**.
     Go to 5.

alternatively

1   Click [**Classfications**] in area (**1**).
2   Select the **Node Classifications** folder in area (**2**).
3   Go to **Create | Classifications | Node Classification**
     or key command [**Ctrl**] + [**Shift**] + [**N**].
     Go to 5.

alternatively

3   Click on any empty space in area (**3**).
4   Right-click and select **New Classification...**

The **New Classification** dialog box now appears:

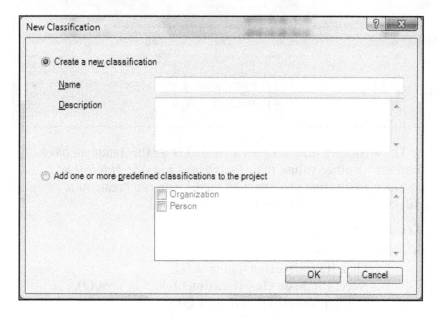

You can choose between creating your own new Classification or using one of NVivo's templates.

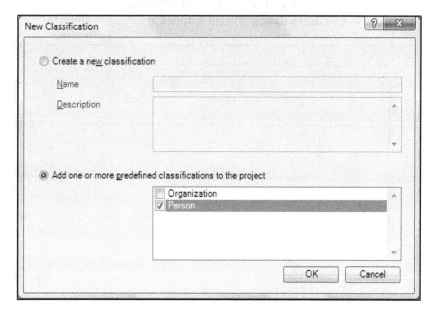

5 This example uses the template *Person.* Click [**OK**].

The result appears like this in area **(3)**:

The attributes that have been created from this template have initially no other values than *Unassigned* and *Not Applicable*.

The classification can easily be edited. You can create new attributes and you can delete those not needed.

Creating an Attribute

♦ **Follow These Steps**
    1   Click [**Classfications**] in area **(1)**.
    2   Select the **Node Classifications** folder in area **(2)**.
    3   Select a Classification in area **(3)**.
    4   Go to **Create | Classifications | Attributes**
        or key command [**Ctrl**] + [**Shift**] + [**N**]
        or right-click and select **New Attribute...**

The **New Attribute** dialog box now appears:

    5   Type a name (compulsory) and a description (optional) and select the attribute type (Text, Integer, Decimal, Date/Time, Date, Time or Boolean), then [**OK**].

You can also decide which values to assign to the attribute. Use either the **New Attribute** dialog box or the **Attribute Properties** dialog box, under the **Values** tab:

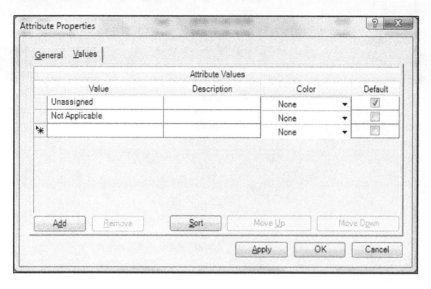

6   The [**Add**] button creates a text box in which you can type new values. Confirm with [**OK**].

Finally, you need to assign the Classification to a node.

♦   **Follow These Steps**
1   Select one or several nodes that shall be assigned a Classification.
2   Right-click and select **Classification** → **<Name of Classification>**.

Alternatively, if you only select *one* node:

♦   **Follow These Steps**
1   Select the node that shall be assigned a Classification.
2   Right-click and select **Node Properties** or key command [**Ctrl**] + [**P**].

The **Node Properties** dialog box appears:

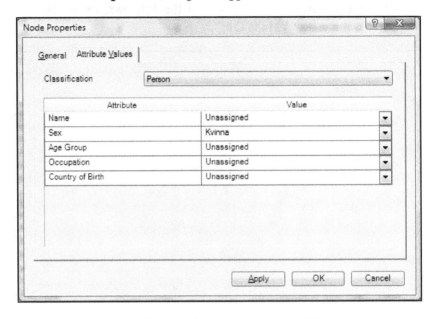

3   Use the **Attribute Values** tab. The **Classification** drop-down list will give you access to all Node Classifications in the project. Select your desired node.

4   In the column *Value* you can use the drop-down list to set individual values to the current node.

5   Confirm with [**OK**].

The overview of source items or nodes on one hand and attributes on the other is called a Classification Sheet. This sheet is a matrix where rows are source items or nodes and columns are attributes. The cells contain the values. A Classification Sheet corresponds to the Casebook used in NVivo 8 and has the same features for importing and exporting data.

Deleting a Classification or an Attribute

♦   **Follow These Steps**

1   Click [**Classifications**] in area (**1**).

2   Select the **Source Classifications** or **Node Classifications** folder in area (**2**).

3   Select the Classification or the Attribute in area (**3**) that you want to delete. Deleting a Classification also deletes its Attributes.

4   Use the [**Del**] key
or go to **Home | Editing | Delete**
or right-click and select **Delete**.

5   Confirm with [**Yes**].

Opening Classification Sheets

♦ **Follow These Steps**

1 Go to **Explore | Classification Sheets → Node Classification Sheets → <Name of Classification>**.

alternatively

1 Select a Classification in area (**3**).

2 Right-click and select **Open Classification Sheet**.

Below is a sample Classification Sheet:

	A : Age Group	B : Country	C : Ever done ...	D : Gender	E : Current pai...	F : Education
1 : Anna	20-29	Aust	Yes	Female	Student	Tertiary
2 : Bernadette	60+	Aust	Yes	Female	Retired	Secondary
3 : Fredric	30-39	Aust	Yes	Male	Management Con	Tertiary
4 : Grace	20-29	Aust	Yes	Female	Marketing	Tertiary
5 : Kalle	60+	Aust	No	Male	Retired	Secondary
6 : Ken	50-59	Aust	Yes	Male	Retired	Secondary
7 : Mary	60+	Aust	Yes	Female	Retired	Secondary
8 : Nick	30-39	Aust	Yes	Male	IT	Tertiary
9 : Peter	30-39	Aust	No	Male	Marketing	Tertiary
10 : Phoebe	30-39	Aust	Yes	Female	Teacher	Tertiary
11 : Sunil	20-29	Aust	Yes	Male	Software Consult	Tertiary

You can do many things with a Classification Sheet: importing, exporting, editing, etc.

Exporting Classification Sheets

A Classification Sheet can be exported as a tabdelimited text-file or an Excel spreadsheet.

♦ **Follow These Steps**

1 Select the Classification Sheet in area (**3**) that you want to export.

2 Go to **External Data | Export → Export Classfication Sheets...**

The **Export Classification Sheets** dialog box now appears:

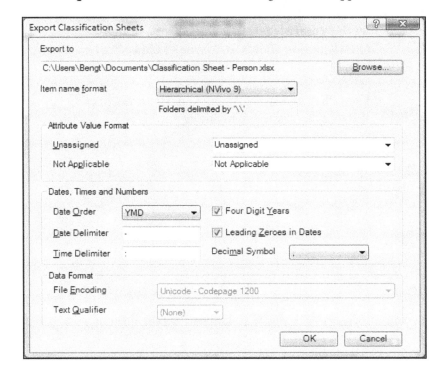

With [**Browse...**] you can decide name, file path and file format.
3   Confirm with [**OK**].

Importing Classification Sheets

You can also import a Classification Sheet as a tab-delimited text-file or an Excel spreadsheet. All nodes, attributes and values are created from the imported file if they do not exist already.

◆   **Follow These Steps**
1   Go to **External Data | Import | Import Classification Sheets**
     or click [**Classifications**] in area (**1**), click on any empty space in area (**3**), right-click and select **Import Classification Sheets...**

The **Import Classification Sheets Wizard – Step 1** now appears:

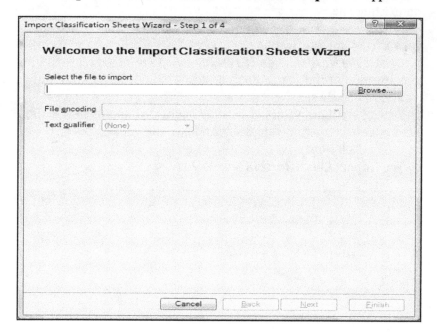

2   With [**Browse...**] you can find the file that you want to
     import.
3   Click [**Next**].
The **Import Classification Sheets Wizard – Step 2** appears:

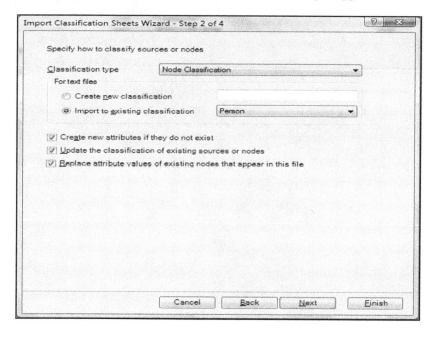

Here you decide if you want to create a new classification or use an existing one.

Create new attributes if they do not exist creates new attributes for the chosen classification.

Update the classification of existing sources or nodes replaces the classification of the source items or nodes that already exist in the location to be chosen.

Replace attribute values of existing nodes that appear in this file determines if imported values shall replace the existing ones.

5   Click **Next**].

The **Import Classification Sheets Wizard** – **Step 3** appears:

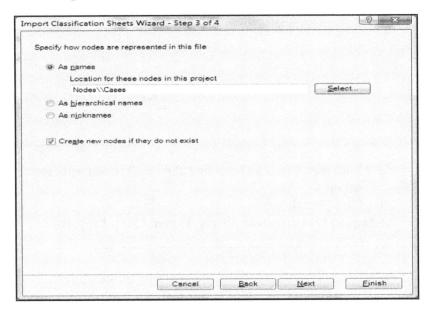

6   Decide the location of the nodes when imported.

7   Click [**Next**].

The **Import Classification Sheets Wizard – Step 4** appears:

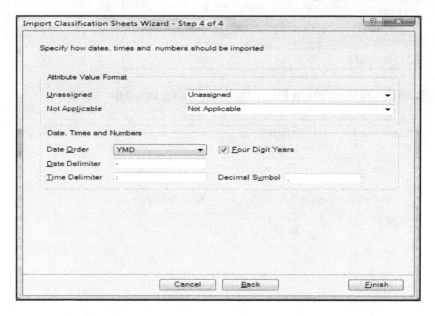

8   Decide the formats of unassigned values, dates, times and numbers.

9   Confirm with [**Finish**].

Hiding/Unhiding Row Numbers (Toggling Function)

♦   **Follow These Steps**

1   Open a **Classification Sheet**.

2   Go to **Layout | Show/Hide | Row IDs**
     or right-click and select **Row → Row IDs**.

Hiding Rows

♦   **Follow These Steps**

1   Open a **Classification Sheet**.

2   Select one row or several rows that you want to hide.

3   Go to **Layout | Show/Hide | Hide Row**
     or right-click and select **Row → Hide Row**.

Hiding/Unhiding Rows with Filters

♦   **Follow These Steps**

1   Open a **Classification Sheet**.

2   Click the 'funnel' in any column head
     or select a column and go to **Layout | Sort & Filter | Filter
     → Filter Row**.

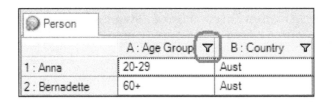

The **Classification Filter Options** dialog box now appears:

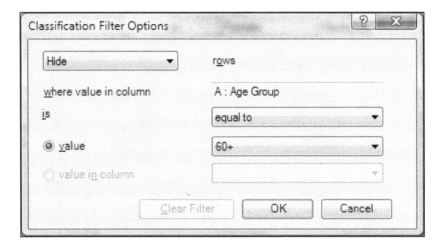

3   Select value and operator for hiding or unhiding. Confirm
    with **[OK]**. When a filter has been applied the funnel
    symbol turns *red*.

To reset a filter select **[Clear Filter]** in the **Classification Filter
Options** dialog box.

Unhiding Rows

♦   **Follow These Steps**
1   Open a **Classification Sheet**.
2   Select one row on each side of the hidden row that you
    want to unhide.
3   Go to **Layout | Show/Hide | Unhide Row**
    or right-click and select **Row → Unhide Row**.

Unhiding All Rows

♦   **Follow These Steps**
1   Open a **Classification Sheet**.
2   Go to **Layout | Sort & Filter | Filter → Clear All Row
    Filters**
    or right-click and select **Row → Clear All Row Filters**.

Hiding/Unhiding Column Letter (Toggling Function)

♦ **Follow These Steps**
1 Open a **Classification Sheet**.
2 Go to **Layout | Show/Hide | Column IDs**
   or right-click and select **Column → Column IDs**.

Hiding Columns

♦ **Follow These Steps**
1 Open a **Classification Sheet**.
2 Select one column or several columns that you want o hide.
3 Go to **Layout | Show/Hide | Hide Column**
   or right-click and select **Column → Hide Column**.

Unhiding Columns

♦ **Follow These Steps**
1 Open a **Classification Sheet**.
2 Select a column on each side of the hidden column that you want to unhide.
3 Go to **Layout | Show/Hide | Unhide Column**
   or right-click and select **Column → Unhide Column**.

Unhiding All Columns

♦ **Follow These Steps**
1 Open a **Classification Sheet**.
2 Go to **Layout | Sort & Filter | Filter → Clear All Column Filters**
   or right-click and select **Column → Clear All Column Filters**.

Transposing the Classification Sheet (Toggling Function)

Transposing means that rows and columns switch places.

♦ **Follow These Steps**
1 Open a **Classification Sheet**.
2 Go to **Layout | Transpose**
   or right-click and select **Transpose**.

Moving a Column Left or Right

♦ **Follow These Steps**
1 Open a **Classification Sheet**.
2 Select the column or columns that you want to move. If you want to move more than one column they need to be adjacent.
3 Go to **Layout | Rows & Columns | Column → Move Left/Move Right**.

Resetting the Classification Sheet

◆ **Follow These Steps**

1 Open a **Classification Sheet**.
2 Go to **Layout | Tools | Reset Settings**
or right-click and select **Reset Settings**.

11. HANDLING BIBLIOGRAPHIC DATA

This chapter is about importing bibliographic data stored in certain selected reference handling software. The file formats that can be imported to NVivo are: .XML for EndNote and .RIS for Zotero and RefWorks.

We describe importing data to NVivo which has been exported from EndNote.

Importing Bibliographic Data

◆ **Follow These Steps**

1   Select and highlight the references from EndNote that you want to export. In EndNote go to **File → Export...** Choose XML as the file format and check *Export Selected References.* Decide file name and file location.

2   In NVivo go to **External Data | Import | Bibliographic Data**. With the file browser you will find the XML file. Click [**Open**].

The **Import Bibliographic Data** dialog box now appears:

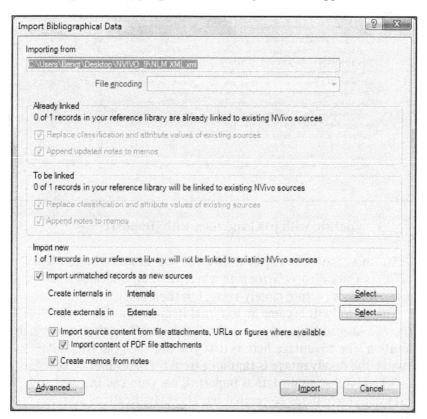

If the references do not already exist in NVivo, the sections *Already linked* and *To be linked* are dimmed.

In the section *Import new* there are several options:

- *Import unmatched records as new sources* means that new records will be be stored as Internals when you import full text material (PDFs) or Externals if there are links to external targets .
- *Import source content from file attachments, URLs or figures where available* means that file attachments, URLs or figures will be imported as an Internal source item.
- *Import content of PDF file attachments* means that attached PDF files will be imported as an Internal source item.
- *Create memos from notes* means that the contents of the Notes-field in the EndNote record will become a memo linked from the source item.

The [**Advanced**] button gives access to the following list of records, where you can choose if values for a certain record shall be replaced or if the Notes-field shall be imported:

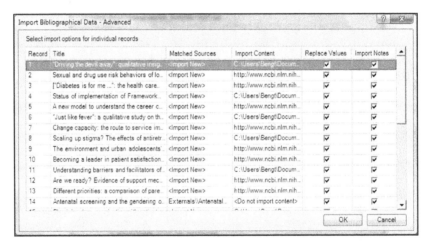

3   Confirm with [**OK**] and then with [**Import**].

The most common way to store a PDF file in an EndNote library (.ENL) is a so-called *relative link* where the PDF is located under a given folder structure closely related to the library.

The record will become an external item with a link to the PDF if the PDF instead is stored as an *absolute link* and retains its original location. The advantage here is that you can open the file in its layout; the disadvantage is that an external PDF cannot be coded.

When bibliographic data is imported, not only can internal and external source items be created but also Classifications and Attributes.

Each Reference Type in EndNote will become a classification and the fields will become attributes. The contents in a field for individual records will become its value. All fields will be represented except the Abstract field which is instead placed in the item's Description.

Source Classifications						
Name /	Created On		Created By	Modified On	Modified By	
Journal Article	2010-11-05 09:31		BME	2010-11-05 12:29	BME	
Name	Type	Created On	Create	Modified On		Modified
Author	Text	2010-11-05 09:31	BME	2010-11-05 09:31		BME
Year	Text	2010-11-05 09:31	BME	2010-11-05 09:31		BME
Title	Text	2010-11-05 09:31	BME	2010-11-05 09:31		BME
Journal	Text	2010-11-05 09:31	BME	2010-11-05 09:31		BME
Volume	Text	2010-11-05 09:31	BME	2010-11-05 09:31		BME
Issue	Text	2010-11-05 09:31	BME	2010-11-05 09:31		BME
Pages	Text	2010-11-05 09:31	BME	2010-11-05 09:45		BME
Start Page	Text	2010-11-05 09:31	BME	2010-11-05 09:45		BME

Exporting Bibliographic Data

You can also export bibliographic data from NVivo to reference handling software. Exporting to EndNote requires the .XML format and export to Zotero and RefWorks requires the .RIS format.

♦ **Follow These Steps**
1 Click [**Sources**] in area (**1**).
2 Select the **Internals** or **Externals** folder in area (**2**), or the subfolder with the source items you want to export.
3 Select the source item or items in area (**3**) that you want to export.
4 Go to **External Data | Export | Export → Export Bibliographical Data**
or right-click and select **Export → Export Bibliographical Data**.

Alternatively, you can also export data from a classification.

♦ **Follow These Steps**
1 Click [**Classifications**] in area (**1**).
2 Select the **Source Classifications** folder in area (**2**).
3 Select the Classification(s) in arca (**3**) that you want to export.
4 Go to **External Data | Export | Export → Export Bibliographical Data**
or right-click and select **Export → Export Bibliographical Data**.
5 Decide file name and file location and make sure that the file format is .XML for EndNote and .RIS for Zotero and RefWorks.
6 Importing to EndNote applies **File → Import...** and the Import Option *EndNote generated XML*.

12. ABOUT DATASETS

This section deals with data that originates from both multiple-choice questions and open-ended questions. A dataset is a source item in NVivo created when structured data is imported. Structured data is organized in records (rows) and fields (columns). The structured data formats that NVivo can import as datasets are Excel spreadsheets, tab-delimited text files and database-tables compatible with Microsoft's Access. A dataset in NVivo is presented in a built-in reader that can display data in both a table format and in a form format. The reader makes it much easier to work on the computer and read and analyse data.

A dataset has two types of fields (columns), namely Classifying and Codable.

Classifying is a field with demographic content of a quantitative nature, often the result of multiple choice questions. The data in these fields is expected to correspond to nodes, attributes, and values.

Codable is a field with 'open ended content' like qualitative data. The data in these fields should typically be the subject of topic coding.

Datasets can only be created when data is imported. Data is arranged in the form of a matrix where rows are records and columns are fields. Typically, respondents are rows, columns are questions and cells are answers.

Importing Datasets

◆ **Follow These Steps**
   1   Go to **External Data | Import | Dataset**
      Default folder is **Internals**.
      Go to 5.
   alternatively
   1   Click [**Sources**] in area (**1**).
   2   Select the **Internals** folder in area (**2**) or its subfolder.
   3   Go to **External Data | Import | Dataset**.
      Go to 5.
   alternatively
   3   Click on any empty space in area (**3**).
   4   Right-click and select **Import Internals → Import Dataset...**

The **Import Dataset Wizard** - **Step 1** now appears:

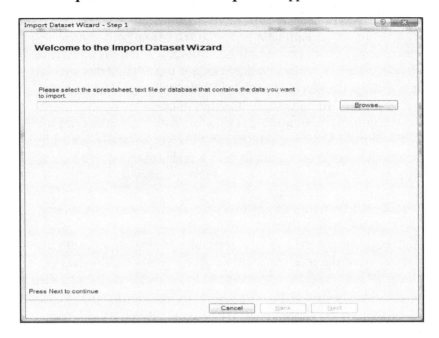

5 With the **[Browse]** button you will find the data file that
   you want to import. The filebrowser only displays file
   formats that can be imported as datasets.

6 Confirm with **[Open]**.

7 Click **[Next]**.

The **Import Dataset Wizard** - **Step 2** appears:

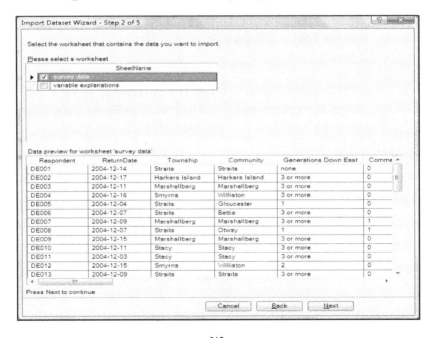

The upper section of the dialog box, SheetName, displays the two sheets of the Excel workbook: survey data and variable explanations. Select a sheet and its contents are displayed under Data Preview. The first 25 records of each are displayed. We select the sheet *survey data*.

8 Click [**Next**].

The **Import Dataset Wizard – Step 3** appears:

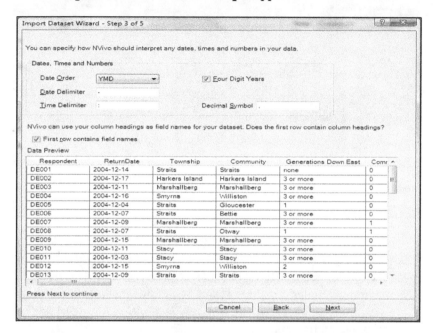

You can verify the Time and Date formats and the Decimal symbol against the information displayed in the Data Preview.

It is important that the field names of imported data are only in the first row. Certain datasheets have field names in two rows and if so then the two rows must be merged. If you uncheck the option *First row contains field names* the row instead will contain column numbers.

9 Click [**Next**].

The **Import Dataset Wizard – Step 4** appears:

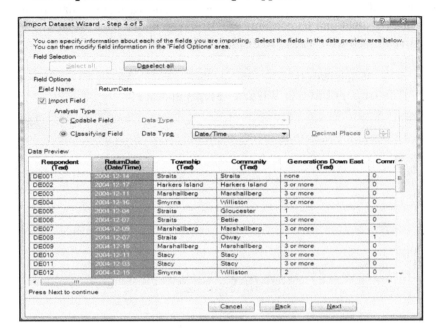

You must assign each column being either a *Codable Field* or a *Classifying Field*. Select one column at a time by clicking the column head (or browse with [**Right**] or [**Left**]) in the Data Preview section. Use the options under *Analysis Type*. The default mode is Classifying for all columns. Unchecking the *Import Field option* for a certain column prevents its import.

   10   Click [**Next**].

The **Import Dataset Wizard – Step 5** appears:

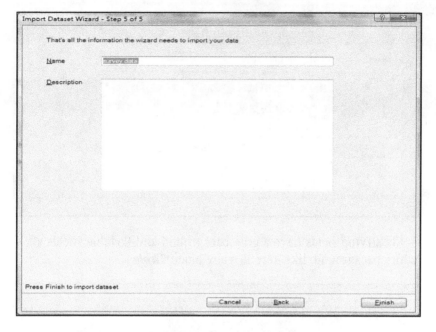

11   Type a name (compulsory) and a description (optional).
     Confirm with **[Finish]**.

A successful import creates a dataset and when it opens in area
(4) and view mode *Table* it appears like this:

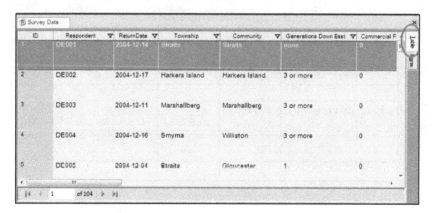

NVivo has created a new leftmost column, ID. A dataset cannot be
edited nor can you create or delete rows or columns. The buttons
down left are for browse buttons between records.

View mode *Form* displays one record at a time:

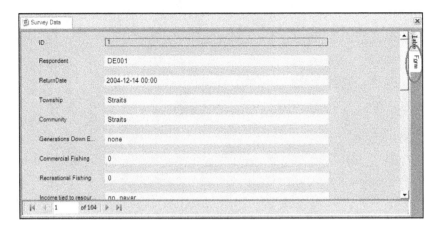

Classifying fields have a grey background and Codable filelds a white background, like here in view mode *Table*:

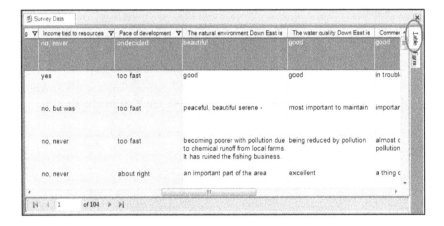

Or here in view mode *Form*:

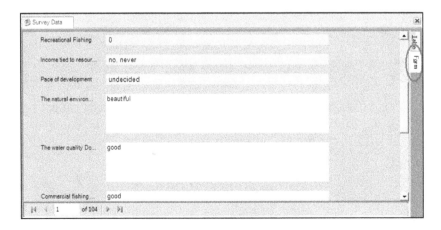

In the **Dataset Properties** dialog box you can do certain modifications to a dataset's presentation:

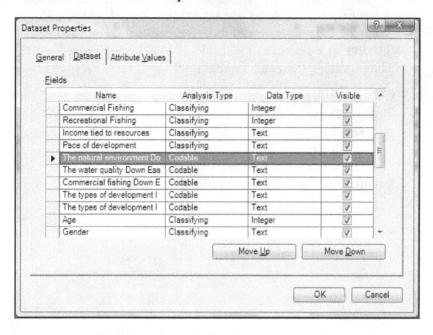

You can change names of a field, hide a field or move a field, but you cannot change Analysis Type or Data Type.

Alternatively, such modifications can also be made directly in a dataset, view mode *Table*. All rules are as described for a Classification Sheet (see page 133), and for Matrices (see page 199), including the use of filters apply to datasets.

Exporting Datasets

Datasets can be exported like other project items.
♦ **Follow These Steps**
1 Click [**Sources**] in area **(1)**.
2 Select the **Internals** folder in area **(2)** or its subfolder.
3 Select the dataset in area **(3)** that you wanr to export.
4 Go to **External Data | Export | Export → Export Dataset...** or key command [**Ctrl**] + [**Shift**] + [**E**] or right-click and select **Export → Export Dataset...**
The **Export Options** dialog box now appears.
5 Select applicable options and click [**OK**]. Then a file browser opens and you can decide file name, file location, and file type. Possible file formats are: Excel, textfile and HTML.
6 Confirm with [**Save**].

Coding Datasets

Coding datasets applies all the common rules: select text in codeable fields, right-click and select **Code Selection → Code Selection At New Node** or **Code Selection At Existing Nodes**.

All coding in a dataset can be explored like in other project items including coding stripes and highlighting.

Autocoding Datasets

◆ **Follow These Steps**

1 Select a dataset in area (**3**) that you want to autocode or click in the open dataset in area (**4**).

2 Go to **Analyze | Coding | Autocode**.

The **Autocode Dataset Wizard – Step 1** now appears:

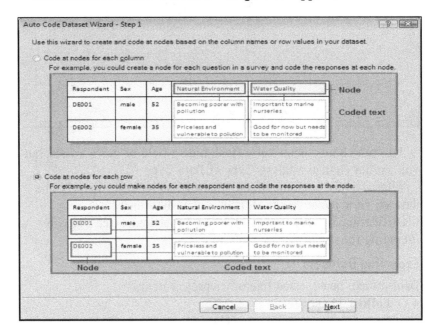

4 Select *Code at nodes for each row*, then click [**Next**].

The **Autocode Dataset Wizard** – **Step 2** appears:

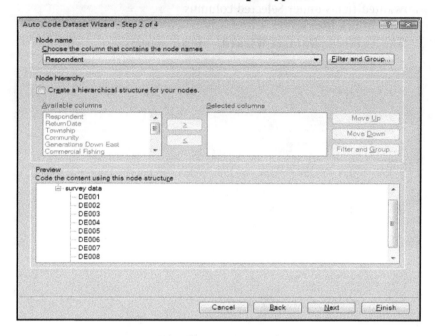

You can decide which fields will become nodes by clicking on a field at *Available Columns* and then by clicking [>] the fields are transferred to *Selected Columns*. Preview displays the node hierarchy that will be created. In our example we only select the column *Respondent*.

4   Click [**Next**].

The **Autocode Dataset Wizard** – **Step 3** appears:

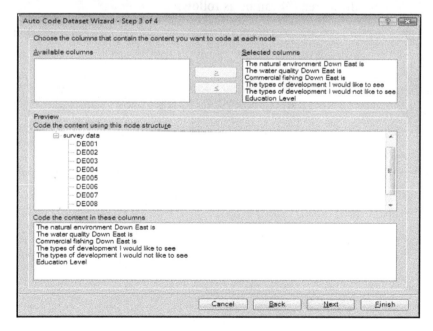

All *Codable* fields are displayed and you can deselect the unwanted fields under Selected columns.

    5   Click [**Next**].

The **Autocode Dataset Wizard – Step 4** appears:

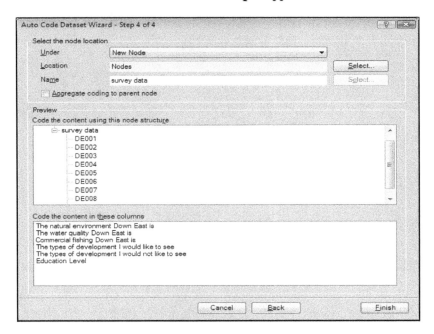

You can now decide the name and location of the new nodes. In our example the location is **Nodes\\Survey Data**.

    6   Confirm with [**Finish**].

The result in area (**3**) can be as follows:

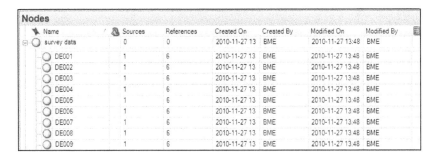

Classification of Datasets

From a dataset you can create and classify nodes based on the Classifying fields. From the beginning there must be at least one existing Node Classification in the project.

If we classify existing nodes (created from autocoding) these nodes must be classified using the same Classification (possibly without Attributes and Values) applied in Stage 2 below.

♦ **Follow These Steps**

1 Select all nodes in area (**3**) that you want to classify. Use [**Ctrl**] + [**A**] or select the first node in the list, then hold down [**Shift**] and click the last node in the list.

2 Right-click and select **Classification → <Name of Classification >**.

The classification from the Dataset is then carried out like this:

♦ **Follow These Steps**

1 Select the dataset in area (**3**) with the data that you want to use for classifying the nodes in question
or click on the open dataset in area (**4**).

2 Go to **Analyze | Classification → Classify Nodes from Dataset**.

The **Classify Nodes from Dataset Wizard – Step 1** now appears:

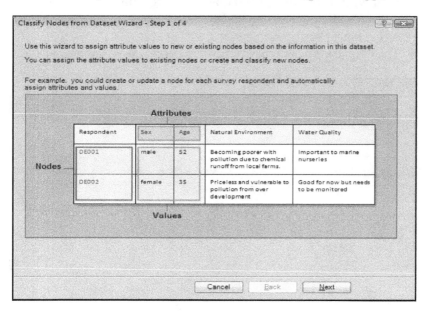

3 Click [**Next**].

The **Classify Nodes from Dataset Wizard** – **Step 2** appears:

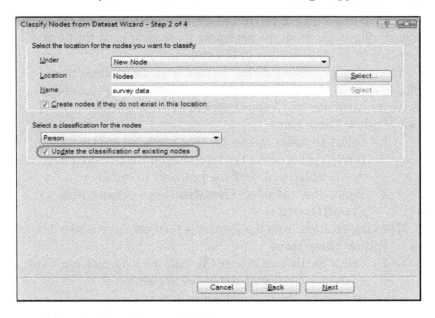

You can now decide if you want to use a new or existing location for the nodes. In our example we will classify the nodes that were created with Autocoding. Therefore it is important to check *Update the classification of existing nodes.*

    4   Click [**Next**].

The **Classify Nodes from Dataset Wizard** – **Step 3** appears:

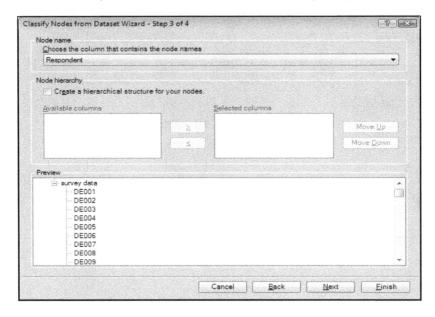

5 We select the column *Respondent* to create the nodes. Click
[**Next**].
The **Classify Nodes from Dataset Wizard – Step 4** appears:

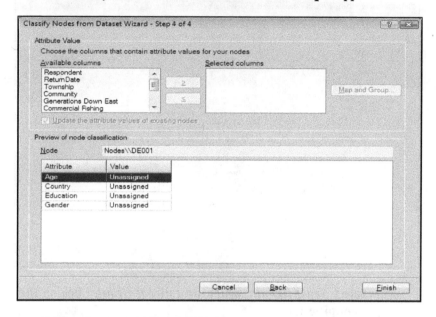

All Classifying fields are listed in the left box, *Available columns*,
and by clicking on a field name and then on [≥] the field names are
transferred to the right box, *Selected columns*. In the section Preview
the result from the topmost node is displayed.
6 Click [**Finish**].

Map and Group

We return to the **Classify Nodes from Dataset Wizard – Step 4**
above. The [**Map and Group**] button can be used to move (or map)
the content from one column to another. There is also an option to
group discrete numerical values as intervals, typically discrete ages
of people to age groups.

♦ **Follow These Steps**
1 In **Classify Nodes from Dataset Wizard – Step 4** the field
   Age has been moved to the right box, Selected columns.

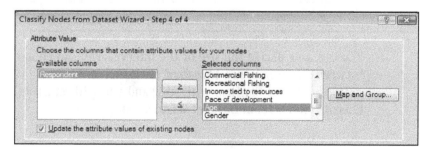

2   Highlight *Age* and click [**Map and Group**].
The **Mapping and Grouping Options** dialog box now appears:

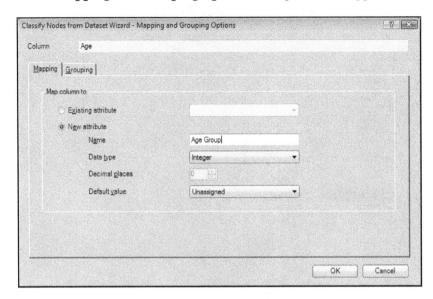

3   Select *New Attribute* which we call *Age Group*. Click on the
    Grouping tab.

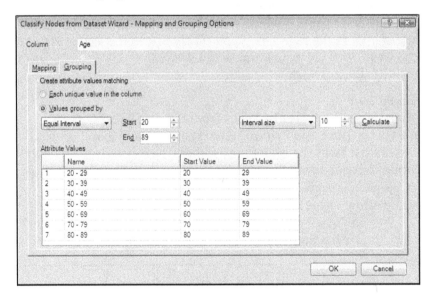

4   You can now decide the size of the interval. You can choose
    between *Equal Interval, Standard Deviation* or *User-
    defined Interval.* Confirm with [**OK**] and you will return to
    Classify Nodes from Dataset Wizard – Step 4.

154

13. ABOUT CODING

Coding data is a similar activity as when you are indexing records in a database. Coding is about associating data with terms from a set of terms, key words, or nodes. People who index scientific databases refer to terminologies as a controlled vocabulary which characterizes and structures database records. Coding large amounts of text, which is usually the case when working with qualitative studies, is a similar form of controlled vacabulary.

A certain difference is that the item which is subject to coding can be any piece of data, even something as small as a single word from a document or single frame from a video. The subject for coding can be an element such as a single letter, a word, a paragraph, a table or an image but can also be a complete document or video.

Nodes are the set of conceptual terms that you will code at. One usually says that you are coding a certain text element at a certain node.

As arguably the most important function of qualitative data analysis software, NVivo offers a variety of methods for coding data:
- The Quick Coding Bar
- Drag-and-drop
- Right-click
- The main menu
- Autocoding
- Paragraph coding
- In Vivo coding
- Query results

Here follows some basic definitions used both in the NVivo commands and in our instructions:

Sources implies that the entire source item is coded.

Selection implies that a selected section in a source item is coded.

Existing Nodes implies that the **Select Project Items** dialog box will appear for selection of one or several nodes.

New Node implies that the **New Node** dialog box will appear and you create and code at a new node directly.

Current Node implies that you code at the node or the nodes that were latest used.

In Vivo implies that you instantly create a node in the **Nodes** folder with the same name as the selected text (max 256 characters).

The Quick Coding Bar

The Quick Coding Bar can be moved around on the screen or be positioned in the lower part of area (4). You can toggle hiding/unhiding and docked/floating by going to **View** | **Workspace** | **Quick Coding** and the options **Hide, Docked** and **Floating**.

The **Quick Coding Bar** is active as long as a selection has been made in a source item or in a node.

The drop-down list at **In** has three options: *Nodes, Relationships* and *Nicknames*. The first time in a new work session you normally select *Nodes* and then click on the first [...] button that now displays the **Select Location** dialog box. From here you can select among node folders and parent nodes. After selecting your nodes, relationships, or nickname, proceed to the dropdown list at **Code At**. This list contains all nodes at the selected location in alphabetic order. You can also use the second [...] button that opens the **Select Project Items** dialog box thus giving access to all nodes. You can select more than one node to code at. You can also create a new node by typing its name in the left text box. The location of this new node is determined by the setting in the left textbox **In**. Key command [**Qtrl**] + [**Q**] positions the cursor in the right text box **Code At**.

The **Code At** drop-down list saves the names of the last nine nodes used during an ongoing work session. You find this list below a divider and in the order they were last used.

Quick Coding bar has the following functions:
- The button **Code at Current Nodes** or [Ctrl] + [F9].
- The button **Uncode at Current Nodes** or [**Ctrl**] + [**Shift**] + [**F9**].
- The button **In Vivo Coding** or [Ctrl] + [F8].

Drag-and-Drop

♦ **Follow These Steps**
1 Click [**Sources**] in area (**1**).
2 Select the folder in area (**2**) with the source item that you want to code.
3 Open the source item in area (**3**) that you want to code.
4 Select the text or image that you want to code.
5 Click [**Nodes**] in area (**1**) and select the folder with the nodes that you want to code at.
6 With the left mousebutton pressed, drag the selection from the source item to the node that you want to code at.

This method is probably the fastest and easiest coding method. Using this method and a customized screen is very productive:
View | **Workspace** | **Detail View** → **Right** and
View | **Workspace** → **Navigation View**
supports drag-and-drop (see page 35).

Right-Click, Menus, or Key Commands

Coding a Source Item
♦ **Follow These Steps**
1   Click [**Sources**] in area (**1**).
2   Select the folder in area (**2**) with the source item that you want to code.
3   Select the source item or items in area (**3**) that you want to code.
4   Go to **Analyze | Coding | Code Sources At** → <select>
     Existing Nodes   [**Ctrl + [F5]**
     New Node   [**Ctrl + [F6]**
alternatively
4   Right-click and select
     Code Sources → <select>
     Code Sources At Existing Nodes   [**Ctrl + [F5]**
     Code Sources At New Node   [**Ctrl + [F6]**
     Recent Nodes <select>

Coding a Selection in a Source Item
♦ **Follow These Steps**
1   Click [**Sources**] in area (**1**).
2   Select the the folder in area (**2**) with the source item that you want to code.
3   Open the source item in area (**3**) that you want to code.
4   Select the text or the section that you want to code.
5   Go to **Analyze | Coding | Code Selection At** → <select>
     Existing Nodes   [**Ctr]l + [F2]**
     New Node   [**Ctrl] + [F3]**
alternatively
5   Right-click and select
     Code Selection → <select>
     Code Selection At Existing Nodes   [**Ctrl] + [F2]**
     Code Selection At New Node   [**Ctrl] + [F3]**
     Code Selection At Current Nodes   [**Ctrl] + [F9]**
     Recent Nodes <select>

     Code In Vivo   [**Ctrl] + [F8]**

Uncoding a Source Item

◆ **Follow These Steps**

1   Click [**Sources**] in area **(1)**.

2   Select the folder in area **(2)** with the source that you want to uncode.

3   Select the source item or items in area **(3)** that you want to uncode.

4   Go to **Analyze | Uncoding | Uncode Sources At →**
    Existing Nodes   **[Ctrl] + [Shift] + [F5]**

alternatively

4   Right-click and select
    Uncode Sources → <select>
    Uncode Sources At Existing Nodes   **[Ctrl + [Shift] + [F5]**
    Recent Nodes <select>

Uncoding a Selection in a Source Item

◆ **Follow These Steps**

1   Click [**Sources**] in area **(1)**.

2   Select the folder in area **(2)** with the source item that you want to uncode.

3   Open the source item in area **(3)** that you want to uncode.

4   Select the text or the section that you want to uncode.

5   Go to **Analyze | Uncoding | Uncode Selection At →**
    Existing Nodes .   **[Ctrl] + [Shift] + [F2]**

alternatively

5   Right-click and select
    Uncode Selection → <select>
    Uncode Selection At Existing Nodes   **[Ctrl] + [Shift] + [F2]**
    Uncode Selection At This Node   **[Ctrl] + [Shift] + [F3]**
    Uncode Selection At Current Nodes   **[Ctrl] + [Shift] + [F9]**
    Recent Nodes <select>

Autocoding

This feature is based on the use of paragraph style names (Heading 1, Heading 2, etc.) to create a hierarchical node structure. The text under each heading becomes the name of the node. If several documents are being autocoded at the same time or separately and they have the same structure of styles and headings then common nodes are created automatically. A practical usage of this feature is when you apply a custom Word template with an established style set as a questionnaire for interviews.

◆ **Follow These Steps**

1 Click [**Sources**] in area **(1)**.
2 Select the folder in area **(2)** with the source items that you want to autocode.
3 Select the source item or items in area **(3)** that you want to autocode.
4 Go to **Analyze | Code | Autocode**
   or right-click and select **Autocode...**

The **Auto Code** dialog box now appears:

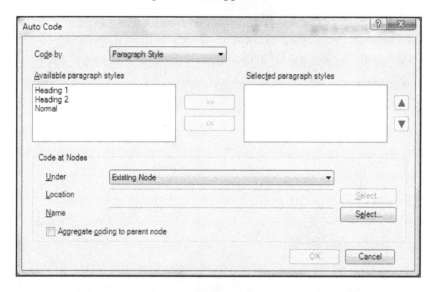

First, you need to decide which paragraph template should become the base for the new node structure. NVivo will find all existing paragraph style templates in any Word document. The templates are selected with the [>>] button and are then transferred to the right textbox. The option *Existing Node* allows you to select the location for the new nodes. If you select *New Node* then you can name the new node and decide under which existing node it should be located. In either case underlying nodes will be named after the text in the respective paragraph style (Heading 1, Heading 2 etcetera).

If you select **Code** by *Paragraph* each paragraph will be coded separately and the names of the nodes will be the prevailing paragraph number.

5 Confirm with [**OK**].

- ◆ -

It is also possible to autocode transcripts of audio- or video-items. Suppose that we have an audio item and a transcript with two optional columns, Speaker and Organization:

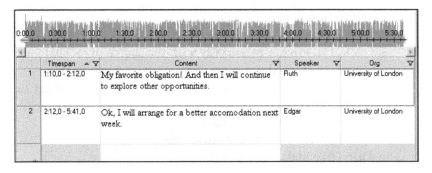

If you select **Code by** *Transcript Fields* autocoding such item will be based on these optional columns which will then create new nodes named after the column contents:

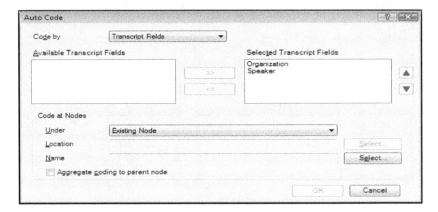

In this example University of London will become a Parent Node to the Child Nodes Ruth and Edgar.

Range Coding

Range coding is another principle for a rational coding of certain items. The basis for range coding is the paragraph number in a document, the row number in a transcript or picture log or the timespan in an audio- or video item.

The available options depend on the type of item that has been selected for range coding. The command is **Analyze | Coding | Range Code** and in this case only existing nodes can be used to code at.

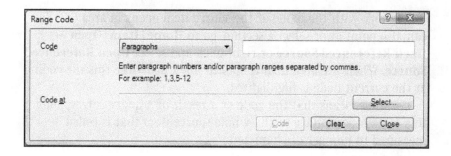

Coding by Queries

Queries can be instructed to save the result. The saved result is a node and is instantly created when the query is run (see Chapter 15, About Queries).

How is Coding Shown?

Opening a Node

◆ **Follow These Steps**

1 Click [**Nodes**] in area (**1**).
2 Select the **Nodes** folder in area (**2**) or its subfolder.
3 Select the node in area (**3**) that you want to open.
4 Go to **Home | Item | Open → Open Node**
   or key command [**Ctrl**] + [**Shift**] + [**O**]
   or right-click and select **Open Node...**
   or double-click the node in area (**3**).

Each open node is displayed in area (**4**) and could therefore be docked or undocked. These windows always have a certain number of view mode tabs on its right side. If the node has only been used to code text then the view mode tabs are: *Summary, Reference* and *Text.*

The *Reference* view mode is the default, automatically selected each time a node is opened:

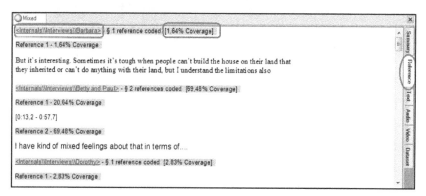

The link with the name of the source item opens in area (4). You can also point at or select a section, go to **Home | Item | Open →
Open Referenced Source** or right-click and select **Open Referenced Source**. When a source item is opened via a node like this the coding at the current node is highlighted.

Coverage means that the node or a result of a query corresponds to a certain percentage of the whole source item that is coded measured in number of characters.

Hiding/Unhiding Reference to Source Items

♦ **Follow These Steps**

1 Open a node.
2 Go to **View | Detail View | Nodes → Coding Summaries**.
3 Uncheck *Sources, References* or *Coverage*.

The option *Sources* hides the reference to source items, coded sections and its coverage.

The option *References* hides information about each coded section and its coverage.

The option *Coverage* hides information about coverage of the source items and its coded sections.

The presentation can be modified in many ways by going to **View | Detail View | Nodes → Coding Context, Coding By Users, Coding Summaries, Coding Excerpt & Node Text**.

The *Summary* view mode displays all coded source items as a list of shortcuts. Each such shortcut can be opened with a double-click and the coded section is highlighted:

Name	In Folder	References	Coverage
Betty and Paul	Internals\Interviews	2	69.48%
Helen	Internals\Interviews	2	22.45%
Maria and Daniel	Internals\Interviews	3	18.87%
Robert	Internals\Interviews	3	11.43%
Survey Responses	Internals\Survey	26	4.62%
Dorothy	Internals\Interviews	1	2.83%
Barbara	Internals\Interviews	1	1.64%

The *Text* view mode displays all coded text source items as thumbnails in the upper part of area (**4**). Clicking on a thumbnail displays the coded section of that source item. Double-clicking the thumbnail opens the whole source item and the coded sections are highlighted:

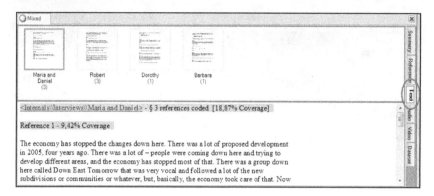

The *Audio* view mode:

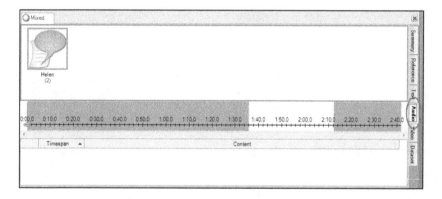

The *Video* view mode:

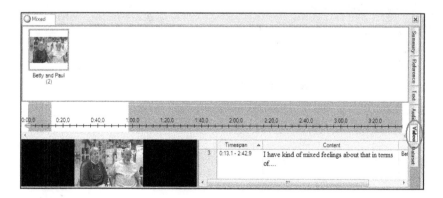

The *Picture* View mode:

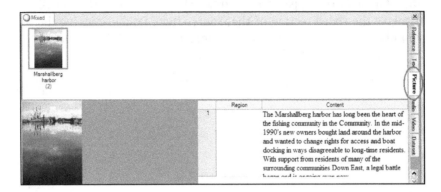

The *Dataset* view mode:

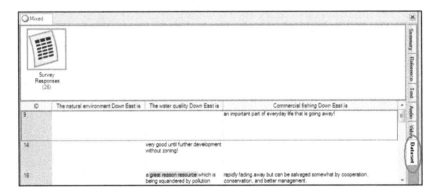

Viewing Coding Excerpt

♦ **Follow These Steps**

1 Open a node.
2 Go to **View | Detail View | Coding Excerpt**.
3 Select *None, First Line* or *All*.

The option *None*.

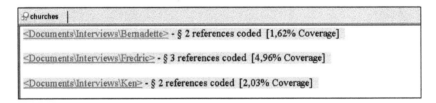

The option *First Line*:

The option *All* is the default and has been shown above.

Viewing Coding Context
♦ **Follow These Steps**
1 Open a node.
2 Select the text or section that you want to show in its context.
3 Go to **View | Detail View | Coding Context**
or right-click and select **Coding Context**.
4 Select *None, Narrow, Broad, Custom...* or *Entire Source*.
Example using the option *Broad*:

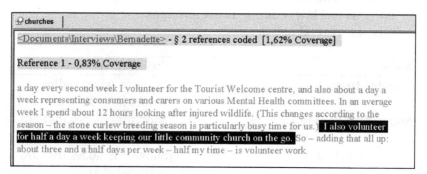

Highlighting Coding
The coded text or section in a source item can be highlighted in brownish color. Settings made are individual to project items and are temporarily saved during a work session, but are reset to none when a project is closed.
♦ **Follow These Steps**
1 Go to **View | Coding | Highlight**.

There are several options:

None	Highlighting is off.
Coding For Selected Items...	Opens Select Project Items showing current nodes, other nodes are dimmed.
Coding for All Nodes	Highlights all nodes that the source item is coded at.
Matches For Query	Highlights the words used by Text Search Queries.
Select Items...	Opens Select Project Items and you can modify selection of nodes.

Coding Stripes

The open document, memo, or node can be made to show the current coding as colored vertical stripes in a separate right hand window. Coding stripes are shown in Read-Only mode or in Edit mode. If you are in Edit mode and start to edit then the coding stripe window and the codning stripes turn grey. Using the Refresh link on top of the window recovers colors and functions of the stripes.

♦   **Follow These Steps**
   1   Go to **View** | **Coding** | **Coding Stripes**.
   There are several options:

None	Coding Stripes are off.
Selected Items...	Is active when coding stripes have been selected.
Nodes Most Coding	Shows the nodes that are most coded at.
Nodes Least Coding	Shows the nodes that are least coded at.
Nodes Recently Coding	Shows the nodes that are recently coded at.
Coding Density Only	Shows only the Coding Density Bar and no nodes.
Selected Items	Opens Select Project Items showing current nodes, other nodes are dimmed.
Show Items Last Selected	Shows the nodes that were last opened.
Number of Stripes...	Selects the number of stripes (7 – 200).

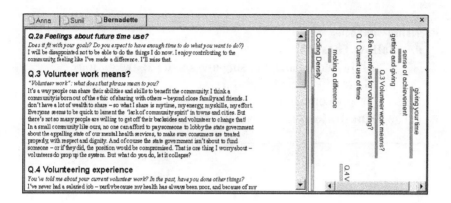

What can you do with Coding Stripes?

When you point and right-click at a certain coding stripe the following options will show: **Highlight Coding, Open Node..., Uncode, Hide Stripe, Show Sub-Stripes, Hide Sub-Stripes** and **Refresh**.

A click on the coding stripe highlights the coded area and double-click opens the node.

By pointing at a coding stripe the node name is shown. By pointing at the Coding Density Bar all node names are shown that are coded at near the pointer.

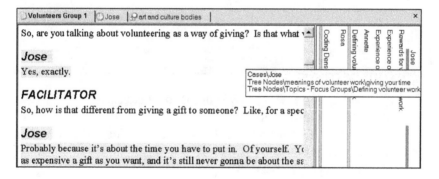

Color Marking of Coding Stripes

The colors of the coding stripes are automatically selected by NVivo. You can also use a custom color scheme, see page 18.

- ♦ **Follow These Steps**
    1 Show coding stripes using any of the above options.
    2 Go to **View | Visualization | Color Scheme → Item Colors**.

Nodes without individual colors in the custom color scheme will be shown without any color.

Printing with Coding Stripes

♦ **Follow These Steps**

1 Show coding stripes using any of the above options.

2 Go to **File | Print | Print...**
or key command **[Ctrl] + [P]**.

The **Print Options** dialog box now appears:

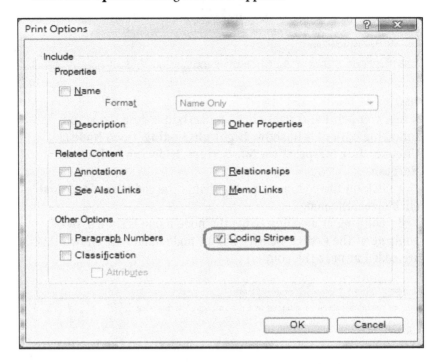

3 The option *Coding stripes* needs to be checked.

4 Confirm with **[OK]**.

Text and coding stripes are printed on separate sheets but together as a pair. A practial measure is therefore to let the printer print two sheets on one page (see page 73).

Charts

Charts is an analytic tool that easily and clearly can illustrate how sources have been coded. The generic way to create Charts is using the Chart Wizard.

♦ **Follow These Steps**

1 Go to **Explore | Visualizations | Charts**.

The **Chart Wizard** – **Step 1** now appears:

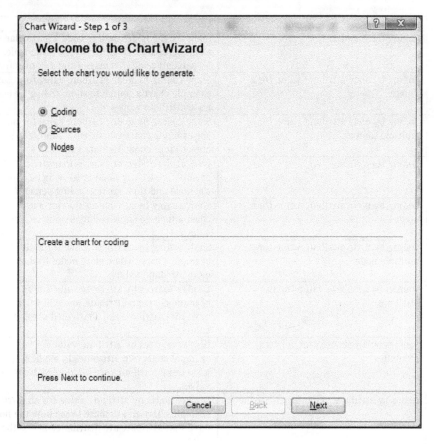

2   Click [**Next**].

The **Chart Wizard** – **Step 2** appears and the options are:

Option	Comments
Coding for a source	Compare the nodes used to code a particular source. For example, chart any source to show the nodes which code it by percentage of coverage or number of references.
Coding by node attribute value for a source	Show coding by node attribute value for a source. For example chart a source to show coding by one or more node attribute values.
Coding by node attribute value for multiple sources	Show coding by node attribute value for multiple sources. For example chart two or more sources to show coding by one or more node attribute values.
Coding for a node	Look at the different sources that atre coded at a node. For example, chart any node to see which sources are coded at the node and their corresponding percentage of coverage.
Coding by node attribute value for a node	Show coding by attribute value for a node. For example, chart a node to show coding by one or more attribute values.
Coding by node attribute value for multiple nodes	Show coding by attribute value for multiple nodes. For example, chart two or more nodes to show coding by one or more attribute values.
Sources by attribute value for an attribute	Display sources by attribute value for an attribute. For example chart an attribute to see how the sources which have that attribute are distributed across the attribute values.
Sources by attribute value for two attributes	Display sources by attribute value for two attributes. For example chart two attributes to see how the sources which have those attributes are distributed across the attribute values.
Nodes by attribute value for an attribute	Display nodes by attribute value for an attribute. For example chart an attribute to see how the nodes which have that attribute are distributed across the attribute values.
Nodes by attribute value for two attributes	Display nodes by attribute value for two attributes. For example chart two attributes to see how the nodes which have those attributes are distributed across the attribute values.

3   Click [**Next**].

The **Chart Wizard** – **Step 3** appears:

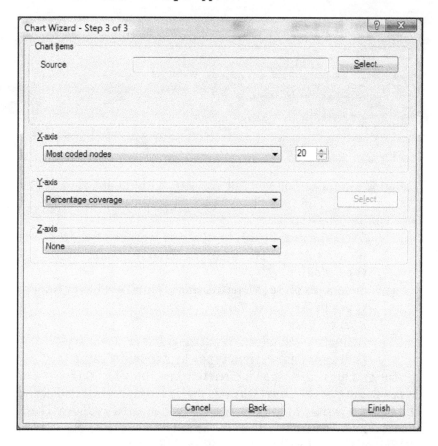

4   Use the [**Select**] button to choose the item that you will
     visualize, then [**Finish**].

The result can be like this:

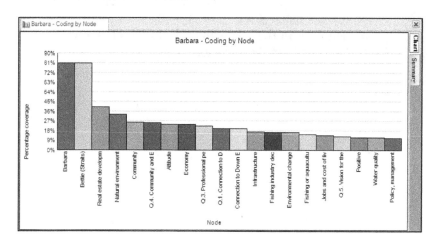

The *Summary* tab displays a list with nodes and their coverage:

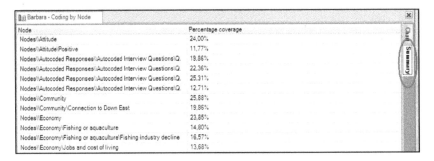

During a work session you can also start with the list view in area
(3).

♦ **Follow These Steps**

1   Select the item in area **(3)** that you want to visualize.

2   Go to **Explore | Visualizations | Chart → Chart <Item
type> Coding**
or go to **Explore | Visualizations | Chart → Chart <Item
type> by Attribute Value**
alternatively
right-click and select **Vizualize → Chart <Item type>
Coding** or **Chart <Item type> by Attribute Value**.

The graphic is then shown directly when you select **Chart <Item
type> Coding** or the **Chart Options** dialog box appears (same box as
the **Chart Wizard** - **Step 2**). From there you proceed as above. These
charts cannot be saved as items in the project but can be exported in
the following file formats: .JPG, .BMP, or .GIF.

♦ **Follow These Steps**

1   Create a Chart.

2   Go to **External Data | Export | Export → Export Chart**
or key command **[Ctrl] + [Shift] + [E]**
or righ-click in the graph and select **Export Chart**.

3   Use the file browser to decide filename and location, then
[Save].

14. FINDING PROJECT ITEMS

This chapter is about how to find project items.

The finding tools are *Find, Advanced Find* and *Grouped Find* and the search results are a list of shortcuts to these items.

Find

The bar **Find** is always just above the List View heading for area **(3)**. This bar can be hidden or unhidden with **View | Workspace | Find** which is a toggling function. The easy function **Find Now** is used for finding names of documents, memos or nodes, not their contents.

- ◆ **Follow These Steps**
  1 At **Look for** you type a whole word or a fragment of a word that is part of the name of an item. Here is free text search applied (not whole words, not case sensitive).
  2 The drop-down list **Search In** is used to select to which folder or folders the search shall be restricted.
  3 Click [**Find Now**].

The results are diplayed in List View, area **(3)**:

This is a list of shortcuts which is indicated by the small arrow in the bottom-right corner of the icons. The list cannot be saved but you can create a set of selected items from the list (see page 46).

Advanced Find

Advanced Find gives increased specificity to any given search..

- **Follow These Steps**
  1. In the **Find** bar go to **Advanced Find**
     or key command [**Ctrl**] + [**Shift**] + [**F**].

The **Advanced Find** dialog box appears.

The drop-down list **Look For** has the following options:

- Sources
- Documents
- Audios
- Videos
- Pictures
- Datasets
- Externals
- Memos
- Nodes
- Relationships
- Matrices
- Source Classifications
- Node Classifications
- Attributes
- Relationship Types
- Sets
- Queries
- Results
- Reports
- Extracts
- Models
- All

As an example of Advanced Find options, you can limit a text search to just the Description box of a certain type of project item.

The Intermediate Tab

The **Intermediate** and **Advanced** tabs are independant of each other. Below is the **Intermediate** tab of the **Advanced Find** dialog box:

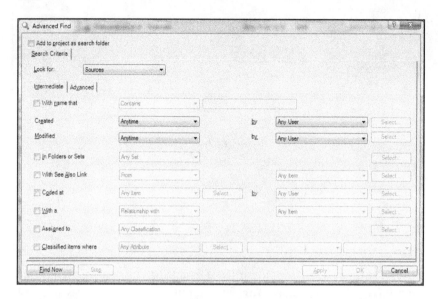

As soon as any option in the Intermediate tab has been choosen the corresponding [**Select...**] button is activated and opens the **Select Project Items** dialog box. The exact shape of this dialog box is determined by the choosen option.

This function can be used to create a list with items matching certain criteria, like:
- Nodes created *last week*
- Nodes that are *Male*
- Memos with a 'See Also Link' from the node *Adventure*
- Documents that are coded at the node *Passionate*
- Nodes that code the document *Volunteers Group 1*
- Sets containing *nodes*

The **Advanced** tab offers other types of criteria:

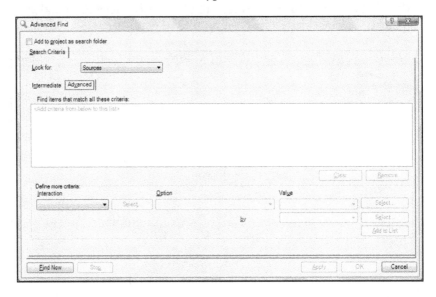

The **Interaction** drop-down list depends on the type of item that you have selected at **Look for**. For example, if *Documents* is selected the drop-down list has the following options:

- Document
- Name
- Description
- Created
- Modified
- Size (MB)
- Attribute

2   Select *Nodes* from **Look for**. In the section *Define more criteria* the drop-down list now has options specifically for nodes.
In this case, select:
Age Group / equals value / 50-59 and the dialog box looks like this:

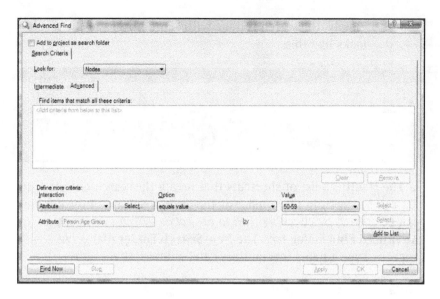

3 Click [**Add to List**] and the search criteria moves to the box **Find items that match all these criteria**.

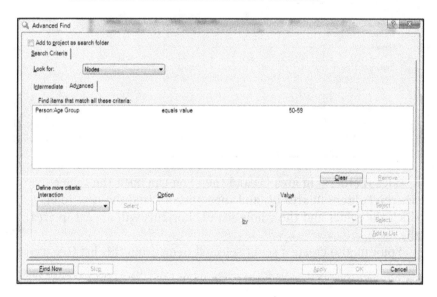

4 You can now add another criterion for example a limitation to women. Then again click [**Add to List**].

5   Finally, the search is done with [**Find Now**] and the result
     looks like this:

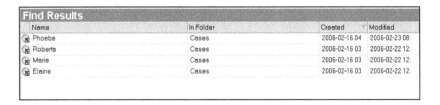

The result is a list of shortcuts that match the search criteria. This
list can be stored in a subfolder of the **Search Folder**. This subfolder
can be created by checking *Add to project as search folder* in the
Advanced Find dialog box. The **New Search Folder** dialog box
appears. Type a name (compulsory) and a description (optional):

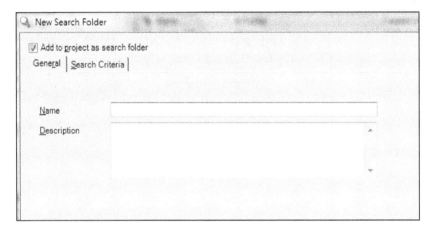

Click [**Folders**] in area **(1)** and then you can open the folder
Search Folders in area **(2)** and then you can find the new folder.
Click the folder and the whole list of shortcuts will appear in area
(3).

You can also create a set of selected items from this list (see page
46).

Group Query

Group Query is a function that makes it possible to create a list of selected items with selected related items. For example the following types of lists can be created:

- Source items and nodes that they are coded at
- Nodes and their coded source items
- Attribute values and matching project items
- Items and their relatonships
- Items and their links
- Items included in models

♦ **Follow These Steps**

1   Go to **Explore | Queries | New Query → Group...**
    Default folder is **Queries**.
    Go to 5.

alternatively

1   Click [**Queries**] in area (**1**).
2   Select the **Queries** folder or its subfolder.
3   Go to **Explore | Queries | New Query → Group...**
    Go to 5.

alternatively

3   Click on any empty space in area (**3**).
4   Right-click and select **New Query → Group...**

The **Group Query** dialog box now appears:

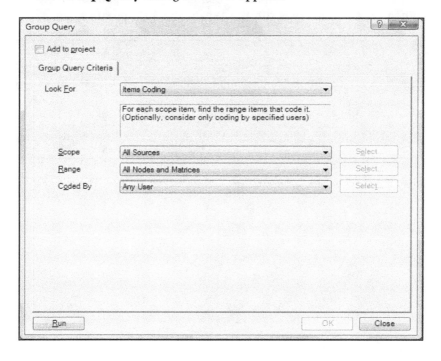

The **Look For** drop-down list has the following options:

- Items Coding
- Items Coded At
- Items by Attitude Value
- Relationships
- See Also Links
- Model Items
- Models

When you have chosen *Selected Items* at **Scope** or **Range** the [**Select...**] button becomes active and it opens the **Select Project Item** dialog box. The exact contents of this dialog box are determined by which of the above options has been chosen.

5   Select *Items Coding* from the **Look For** drop-down list.
6   Select *Selected Items* from the **Scope** drop-down list.
7   Click [**Select...**].
8   Select the **Internals** folder and **Interviews** subfolder in the **Select Project Items** dialog box.
9   Click [**OK**].
10 Select *All Nodes and Matrices* from the **Range** drop-down list.
11 Click [**Run**].

Group Query Results are displayed as an expandable list in area (**3**). This list cannot be saved. The query, however, can be saved as any other queries (see Chapter 17, Common Query Features, page 219). When the saved query is run the expandable list appears again.

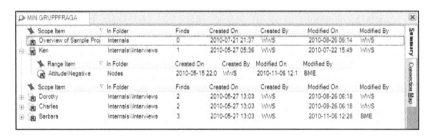

The *Connection Map* tab to the right in area (4) lets you display a circular graph showing the relations between selected source items and selected nodes:

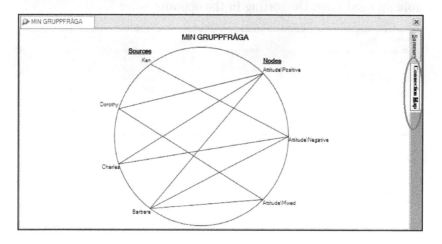

Sorting of Items

This section applies to all items that can be viewed in a list usually in area (3), but sometimes also in area (4). For example, when a node is opened in view mode Summary, a list is shown in area (4).

♦ **Follow These Steps**
   1   Display a list of items in area (3).
   2   Go to **Layout | Sort & Filter | Sort By → <select>**.

The options offered depend on of the type of items in the list. Nodes, for example, can be arranged hierarchically, so for nodes there is a special sorting option, Custom.

♦ **Follow These Steps**
   1   Display a list with Nodes in area (3).
   2   Go to **Layout | Sort & Filter | Sort By → Custom**.
   3   Select the node or nodes that you want to move. If you want to move more than one node they must be adjacent.
   4   Go to **Layout | Rows & Columns | Row → Move Up/ Move Down**
       or key command **[Ctrl] + [Shift] + [U]/ [Ctrl] + [Shift] + [D]**.

This sorting is automatically saved even if you temporarily change the sorting. You can always return to your Custom sorting:

♦ **Follow These Steps**
   1   Display a list of items in area (3).
   2   Go to **Layout | Sort & Filter | Sort By → Custom**.

This command is a toggling function. When you use the command again it sorts in the opposite order.

You can also use the column heads for sorting. Sorting by commands or sorting with column heads always adds a small triangle to the column head in question. Clicking again on this column head turns the sorting in the opposite order.

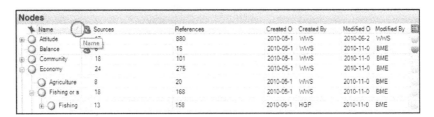

15. ABOUT QUERIES

This chapter is about how to create and run various kinds of queries. You can construct simple queries that find certain items or text elements, or you can construct complex queries that combine search words and nodes or that combine several nodes. The results of queries based on search words and nodes generate new nodes and can be saved as such. There is also a possibility to merge query results with existing nodes.

The query types Text Searches, Coding Queries, Compound Queries and Matrix Coding Queries display results as previews (temporary nodes) or new nodes (saved). Word Frequency Queries display a ranked term list as the result. Group Queries were dealt with in the previous chapter and Coding Comparison Queries are dealt with in Chapter 16, About Teamwork.

Saving a query, editing a query, moving a query to another folder, deleting a query and previewing or saving results are dealt with in Chapter 17, Common Query Features (see page 219).

Text Search Queries

Text Search Queries search for certain words or phrases in a set of items.

◆ **Follow These Steps**
  1   Go to **Explore** | **Queries** | **New Query** → **Text Search...**
       Default folder is **Queries**.
       Go to 5.
  alternatively
  1   Click [**Queries**] in area **(1)**
  2   Select **Queries** folder in area **(2)** or its subfolder.
  3   Go to **Explore** | **Queries** | **New Query** → **Text Search...**
       Go to 5.
  alternatively
  3   Click on an empty space in area **(3)**.
  4   Right-click and select **New Query** → **Text Search...**

The **Text Search Query** dialog box now appears:

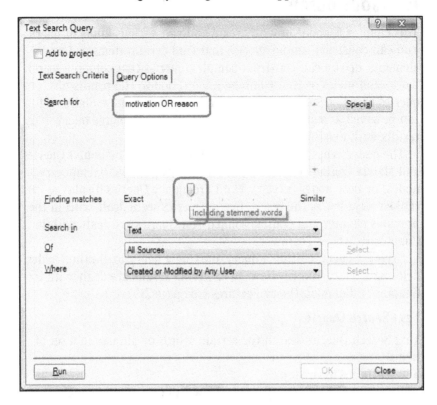

5   Type the search word or the search criteria in the **Search for** text box, for example `motivation OR reason`. Move the slider **Finding matches** over the option *Including stemmed words*, this way the query searches words with same stem as the typed search words. (English, French, Spanish and German only).

When several words are typed in a sequence, e.g. ADAM EVE, the search is made as an OR-combination and when the words are surrounded by quotes, "ADAM EVA", an exact phrase search is run.

184

The slider **Finding matches** has five options:

Position	Comment	Example
1	Exact matches only	sport
2	Exact matches Words with the same stem	sport, sporting
3	Exact matches Words with same stem Synonyms (words with a very close meaning)	sport, sporting, play, fun
4	Exact matches Words with same stem Synonyms (words with a very close meaning) Specializations (words with a more specialized meaning)	sport, sporting, play, fun, running, basketball
5	Exact matches Words with same stem Synonyms (words with a very close meaning) Specializations (words with a more specialized meaning—a 'type of') Generalizations (words with a more general meaning)	sport, sporting, play, fun, running, basketball, recreation, business

The settings 3 – 5 only works for NVivo's text search languages. The text search language options are available when you go to **File → Info → Project Properties,** the **General** tab: *Text Search Language.* If the setting is for *None* then only position 1 can be used but can be combined with the conventional operators under [**Special**].

The [**Special**] button offers the following options:

Option	Example	Comment
Wildcard ?	ADAM?	? represents *one* arbitrary character
Wildcard *	EVA*	* represents *any number* of arbitrary characters
AND	ADAM AND EVA	Both words must be found
OR	ADAM OR EVA	Either word must be found
NOT	ADAM NOT EVA	Adam is found where Eve is not found
Required	+ADAM EVA	Adam is required but Eve is also found
Prohibit	-EVA ADAM	Adam is found where Eve is not found
Fuzzy	ADAM~	Finds words of similar spelling
Near...	"ADAM EVA"~3	Adam and Eve are found within 3 words from each other
Relevance...	ADAM^2EVA	Adam is 2 times as relevant as Eve is

6   Confirm with [**Run**].

The format of the result depends on the settings made under the **Query Options** tab (see page 221).

The *Preview Only* option displays a list of shortcuts in area (4) and can look like this. The **Summary** tab is default:

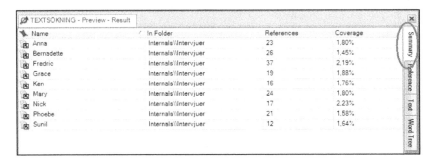

The list of shortcuts can easily be sorted by clicking on the column head. When you double-click on such shortcut the item will open and the search words are highlighted:

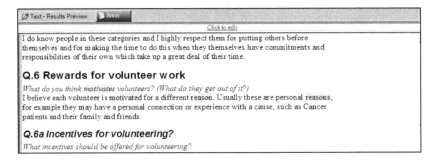

Creating a Set

♦   **Follow These Steps**

1   Select the shortcuts that you want to create as a set.

2   Go to **Create | Collections | Create As Set**.

3   Type a name of the new set and confirm with [**OK**].

alternatively, if you already have a set:

♦   **Follow These Steps**

1   Select the shortcuts that you want to add to a set.

2   Go to **Create | Collections | Add To Set**
    or right-click and select **Add To Set.**

3   Select Set in the **Select Set** dialog box.

4   Confirm with [**OK**].

Creating a Node

♦ **Follow These Steps**

1 Select the shortcuts that you want to create as a node.

2 Right-click and select **Create As → Create As Node...** (selected shortcuts will be merged into one new node) or
right-click and select **Create As → Create As Nodes...** (selected shortcuts will each become a new node).

3 In the **Select Location** dialog box you must determine where the new node or nodes shall be located.

4 Type a name for the new node(s) and confirm with **[OK]**.

Saving Search Results

♦ **Follow These Steps**

1 Select the shortcuts that you want to create as a node.

2 Right-click and select **Store Query Results** (all shortcuts will be merged into one new node) or
right-click and select **Store Selected Query Results** (selected shortcuts will be merged into one new node)

The **Store Query Results** dialog box now appears.

3 Determine the name and location of the new node.

The *Reference* view mode displays 5 words on each side of the search word (Coding Context) and otherwise the view options are the same as for an open node:

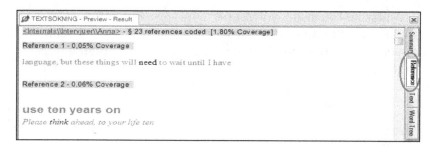

The *Text* view mode is also identical as for an open node:

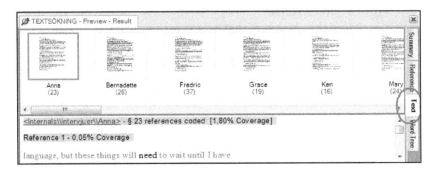

The *Word Tree* view mode is a new feature for text search queries when Query Options is set for Preview:

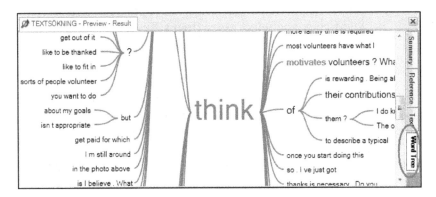

A new Ribbon menu, **Word Tree**, now appears and there you can find a list called Root Term. This list is sorted by frequency, and displays words resulting from the placement of the **Finding matches** slider. Each selected Root Term creates a new Word Tree. You can also decide the number of words (Context Words) that surrounds a Root Term.

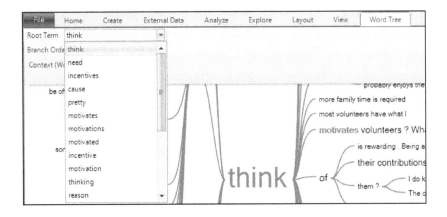

Finally, you can also click any word of the Word Tree and the complete actual branch will be highlighted. Double-clicking these branches opens a preview of the source item.

Coding Queries

Coding Queries are advantageous when you have advanced your project's structure in such a way that you can acquire project insights via complex queries. The following options and functions are explained on page 219 and onwards:

- Automatically select subfolders
- Automatically select hierarchy
- The [**Filter**] button

◆ **Follow These Steps**

1   Go to **Explore** | **Queries** | **New Query** → **Coding...**
     Default folder is **Queries**.
     Go to 5.

alternatively

1   Click [**Queries**] in area (**1**).
2   Select the **Queries** folder in area (**2**) or its subfolder.
3   Go to **Explore** | **Queries** | **New Query** → **Coding...**
     Go to 5.

alternatively

3   Click at an empty space in area (**3**).
4   Right-click and select **New Query** → **Coding...**

The **Coding Query** dialog box now appears:

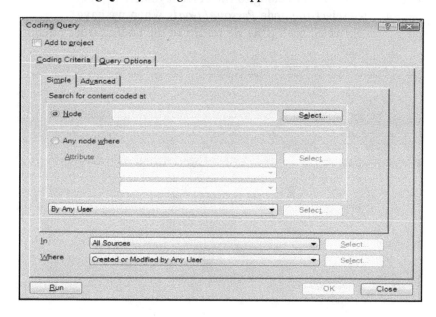

5   Go to the **Criteria** tab and select either the **Simple** tab or the **Advanced** tab.

Example: What motivates people in the age group 30 - 39 to do volunteering? Let's first limit the search to the node *Personal Goals*.

◆ **Follow These Steps**
  1 Select **Coding Criteria → Simple** tab.
  2 Choose *Selected Items* from the drop-down list **In**.
  3 Click the [**Select...**] button.

The **Select Project Items** dialog box now appears:

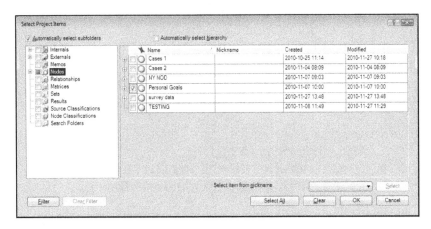

In the left part of the dialog box the whole folder structure of the project is shown and in the right part you can find the items (source items, nodes etc.) that belong to the current folder.

  4 We select the node *Personal Goals*. When we have confirmed with [**OK**] we return to the **Coding Query** dialog box.

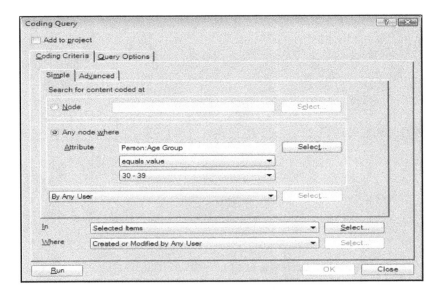

5   Click [**Select...**] at *Any Node Where* and the **Select Project Items** dialog box shows only Classifications and Attributes.

6   Select the Attribute Age Group and the Value 30 – 39. Click [**OK**].

7   Click [**Run**] in the **Coding Query** dialog box.

The format of the result depends on the settings of the **Query Options** tab (see page 221).

Criteria Tab → Advanced Tab

The **Simple** tab and the **Advanced** tab are indpendent of each other. The **Advanced** tab makes more complex search criteria possible. In this example, we want to limit the search to females in the age group 30 – 39 and then search the nodes Personal Goals and Family Values.

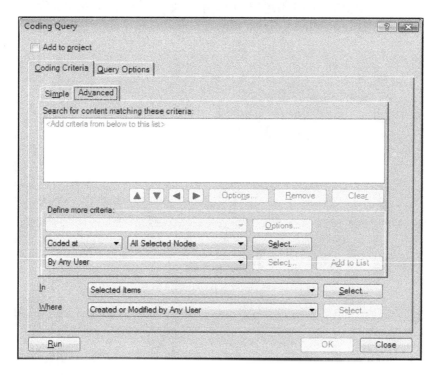

♦   **Follow These Steps**

1   Select **Coding Criteria → Advanced** tab.

2   Under **Define more criteria** choose the option *Coded at* and *Any Node Where*, then the [**Select...**] button.

The **Coding Search Item** dialog box now appears:

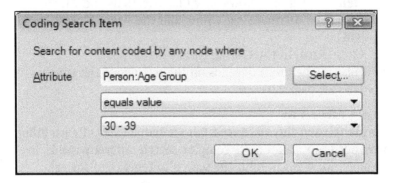

3 Select Attribute and Value *Age Group / equals value / 30-39.*
4 Confirm with **[OK]** and then click **[Add to List]** in the
   Coding Query dialog box.

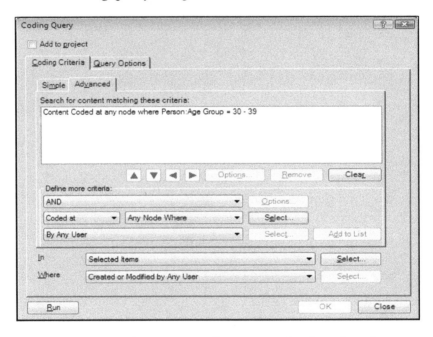

5 Return to the section **Define more criteria**, select the
   operator[1] *AND, Coded at* and *Any Node Where.*
6 Use the **[Select...]** button and select *Gender / equals value /
   Female* in the **Coding Search Item** dialog box.

_____

[1] See page 227 onward for explanations of the other operators on
this drop-down list.

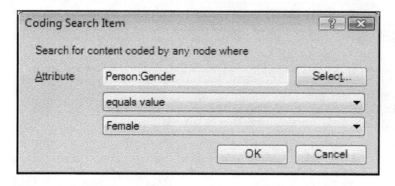

7　Confirm with [OK] and then click [Add to List] in the **Coding Query** dialog box.

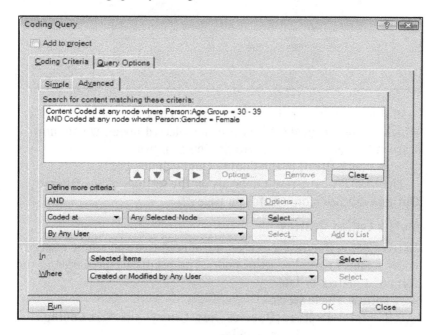

8　Return to the section Define more criteria, select the operator[2] *AND, Coded at* and *Any Selected Node Where.* With the [Select] button you select the two nodes Personal Goals and Family Values.

9　Confirm with [OK] and then click [Add to List] in the **Coding Query** dialog box.

---

[2] See page 227 onward for explanations of the other operators on this drop-down list.

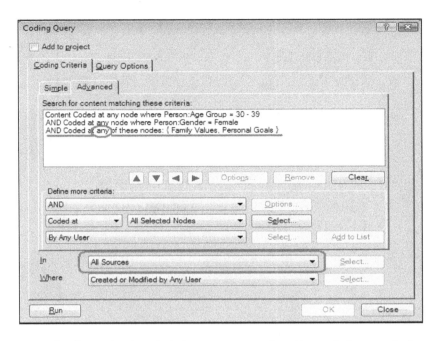

In this last criterion, it is important to select 'Any of these nodes' which means a logical OR between the selected nodes. We are now searchng *All Sources* as the criteria limits anyway.

10 Click [**Run**] in the **Coding Query** dialog box.

The format of the result depends on the settings of the **Query Options** tab. See more on this on page 221.

Matrix Coding Queries

Matrix Coding Queries have been introduced to display how a set of nodes relates to another set of nodes. The results are presented in the form of a matrix or table.

♦ **Follow These Steps**

1 Go to **Explore | Queries | New Query → Matrix Coding...**
Default folder is **Queries**.
Go to 5.

alternatively

1 Click [**Queries**] in area (**1**).
2 Select the **Queries** folder in area (**2**) or its subfolder.
3 Go to **Explore | Queries | New Query → Matrix Coding...**
Go to 5.

alternatively

3 Click on an empty space in area (**3**).
4 Right-click and select **New Query → Matrix Coding...**

The **Matrix Coding Query** dialog box now appears:

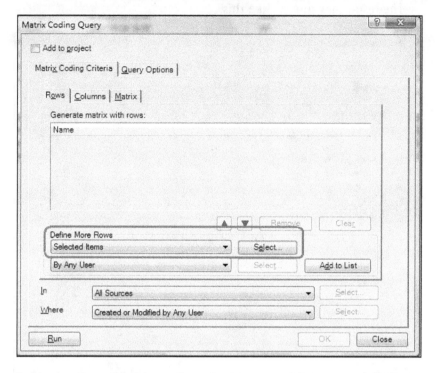

5   Select the **Matrix Coding Criteria** tab and then the **Rows** tab.
6   Choose *Selected Items* from the **Define More Rows** drop-down list.
7   Click **[Select...]**.

The **Select Project Item** dialog box now appears:

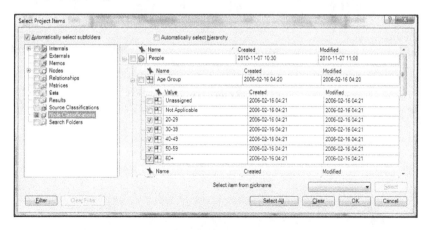

8   Select **Node Classifications\\People\\Age Group** and check the values that you want to use. Click **[OK]**.

9   Click [**Add to List**].

The result may appear like this:

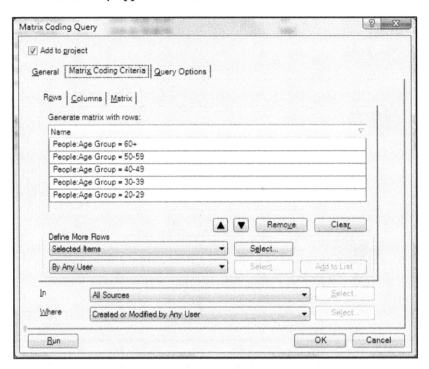

10   Select the **Matrix Coding Criteria** tab and then the
     Columns tab.

11   Choose *Selected Items* from the **Define More Columns** drop-
     down list.

12   Click [**Select...**].

The **Select Project Items** dialog box now appears:

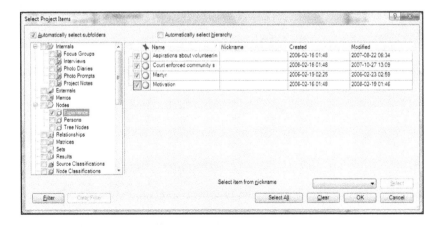

13 Select **Nodes\\Experience** and check the nodes that you want to study. Click **[OK]**.

14 Click **[Add To List]**.

When you have defined the columns the result may be like this:

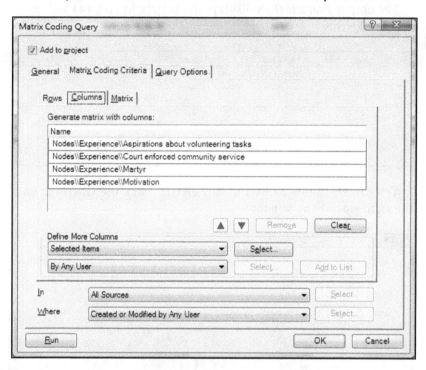

If there are nodes that you would like to delete, select them and click **[Remove]**. The whole list is cleared with **[Clear]**. If you want to change the order then select a node and use the arrow buttons to move up or down.

15 Select the **Matrix Coding Criteria** tab and then the **Matrix** tab.

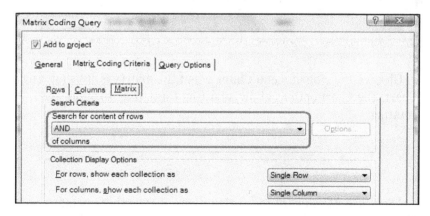

You can now choose operator[3] to use between rows and columns.

16   Click [**Run**] in the **Matrix Coding Query** dialog box.

The format of the result depends on the settings under the **Query Options** tab (see page 221).

The option *Preview Only* displays the matrix in area (**4**) and may appear like this:

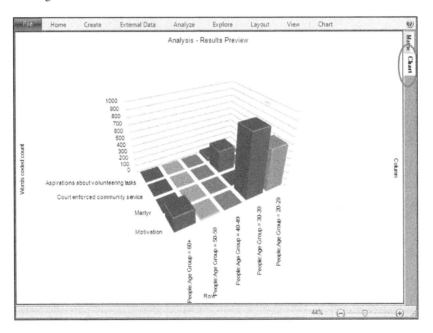

You can also show a Chart of this matrix. Click the *Chart* tab on the right side of the window:

Observe the ribbon menu **Chart** when the matrix is showing as a Chart. The Chart options allow adjusting formating, zooming and rotating.

---

[3] See page 227 onward for explanations of the other operators on this drop-down list.

Opening a Cell

A matrix is a collection of cells. Each cell is a node. You need therefore to study each cell separately.

♦ **Follow These Steps**
1 Open the matrix.
2 Select the cell you want to open.
3 Right-click and select **Open Matrix Cell**
   or double-click the cell.

The cell opens and can be analysed as any other cell. This node is an integral part of the matrix and if you want to save it as a new node then select the whole node in the *Reference* view mode and go to **Analyse | Coding | Code Selection At → New Node** or right-click and select **Code Selection → Code Selections At New Node** or key command **[Ctrl] + [F3]**.

Viewing Cell Content

There are several options to view cell content when cells are not opened.

♦ **Follow These Steps**
1 Open the matrix.
2 Go to **View | Detail View | Matrix Cell Content → <select>**
   or right-click and select **Matrix Cell Content → <select>**
   any of the following options:

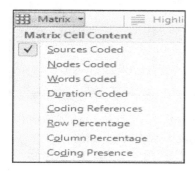

Hiding/Unhiding Row Numbers

♦ **Follow These Steps**
1 Open the matrix.
2 Go to **Layout | Show/Hide | Row IDs**
   or right-click and select **Row → Row Ids**.

Hiding Rows

♦ **Follow These Steps**
1 Open the matrix.
2 Select one or more rows that you want to hide.

3 Go to **Layout | Show/Hide | Hide Row**
   or right-click and select **Row → Hide Row**.

Hiding/Unhiding Rows with Filters
♦ **Follow These Steps**
   1 Open the matrix.
   2 Click the 'funnel' in a certain column head
      or select a column and go to **Layout | Sort & Filter | Filter
      → Filter Row**.

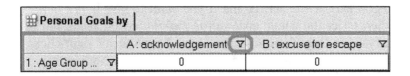

The **Matrix Filter Options** dialog box now appears:

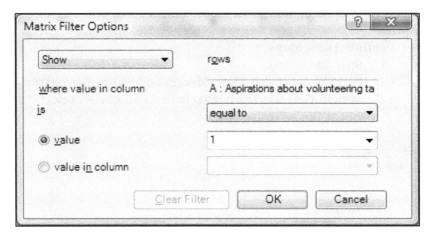

   3 Select value and operator for hiding or unhiding. Confitrm
      with **[OK]**. When a filter is applied the funnel turns *red*.
   To clear a filter use **[Clear Filter]** in the **Matrix Filter Options**
   dialog box.

Unhiding Rows
♦ **Follow These Steps**
   1 Open the matrix.
   2 Select one row on each side of the hidden row that you
      want to unhide.
   3 Go to **Layout | Show/Hide | Unhide Row**
      or right-click and select **Row → Unhide Row**.

Unhiding All Rows

♦ **Follow These Steps**

1   Open the matrix.

2   Go to **Layout | Sort & Filter | Filter → Clear All Row Filters**

or right-click and select **Row → Clear All Row Filters**.

Hiding/Unhiding Column Letters

♦ **Follow These Steps**

1   Open the matrix.

2   Go to **Layout | Show/Hide | Column IDs**

or right-click and select **Column → Column IDs**.

Hiding Columns

♦ **Follow These Steps**

1   Open the matrix.

2   Select one or more columns that you want to hide.

3   Go to **Layout | Show/Hide | Hide Column**

or right-click and select **Column → Hide Column**.

Unhiding Columns

♦ **Follow These Steps**

1   Open the matrix.

2   Select one column on each side of the hidden column that you want to unhide.

3   Go to **Layout | Show/Hide | Unhide Column**

or right-click and select **Column → Unhide Column**.

Unhiding All Columns

♦ **Follow These Steps**

1   Open the matrix.

2   Go to **Layout | Sort & Filter | Filter → Clear All Column Filters**

or right-click and select **Column → Clear All Column Filters**.

Transposing the Matrix

Transposing means that rows and columns are changing places.

♦ **Follow These Steps**

1   Open the matrix.

2   Go to **Layout | Transpose**

or right-click and select **Transpose**.

Moving a Column Left or Right

♦ **Follow These Steps**

1 Open the matrix.
2 Select the column or columns that you want to move. If you want to move more than one column they need to be adjacent.
3 Go to **Layout** | **Rows & Columns** | **Column → Move Left/Move Right.**

Resetting the Whole Matrix

♦ **Follow These Steps**

1 Open the matrix.
2 Go to **Layout** | **Tools** | **Reset Settings**
or right-click and select **Reset Settings**.

Viewing the Cells Shaded or Colored

♦ **Follow These Steps**

1 Open the matrix.
2 Go to **View** | **Detail View** | **Matrix → Matrix Cell Shading → <select>**
or right-click and select **Matrix Cell Shading → <select>**.

Exporting a Matrix

♦ **Follow These Steps**

1 Open or select the matrix.
2 Go to **External Data** | **Export** | **Export Matrix...**
or key command **[Ctrl]** + **[Shift]** + **[E]**
or right-click and select **Export Matrix...**

The **Save As** dialog box appears and you can decide the file name and file location and create a text file or an Excel spreadsheet.

When you view a Chart you can export the image in the following formats: .JPG, .BMP or .GIF.

Convertering a Matrix to Nodes

There are situations when you need to convert cells in a matrix to nodes.

♦ **Follow These Steps**

1 Open or select the matrix.
2 Copy by going to **Home** | **Clipboard** | **Copy**
or key command **[Ctrl]** + **[C]**
or right-click and select **Copy**.
3 Click **[Nodes]** in area **(1)**.
4 Select the **Nodes** folder or its subfolder.
5 Go to **Home** | **Clipboard** | **Paste → Paste**
or key command **[Ctrl]** + **[V]**
or right-click and select **Paste**.

The **Paste** dialog box now appears:

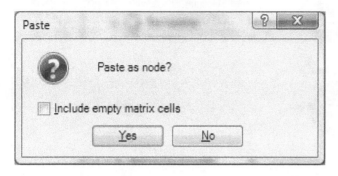

7 Confirm with [**Yes**].

The result is a hierachical node where the Parent node inherits the name of the matrix. The first generation child nodes are the rows and the grandchildren nodes contain contents from each cell.

Converted Matrices				
Name	Sources	References	Created On	Created By
Name of Matrix	7	219	2010-11-17 09:	BME
Anna	1	27	2010-11-17 09:	BME
Job Satisfaction	1	14	2010-11-17 09:	BME
Leisure Activities	1	10	2010-11-17 09:	BME
Salary Importance	1	3	2010-11-17 09:	BME
Bernadette	1	27	2010-11-17 09:	BME
Job Satisfaction	1	14	2010-11-17 11:	BME
Leisure Activities	1	10	2010-11-17 11:	BME
Salary Importance	1	3	2010-11-17 11:	BME

These nodes can then be used for Cluster Analysis (see page 239).

Word Frequency Queries

Word Frequency Queries makes it possible to make a list of the most frequent words in selected items: source items, nodes etc.

♦ **Follow These Steps**

1 Go to **Explore** | **Queries** | **New Query** → **Word Frequency...**
Default folder is **Queries**.
Go to 5.

alternatively

1 Click [**Queries**] in area (**1**).
2 Select **Queries** folder in area (**2**) or its subfolder.
3 Go to **Explore** | **Queries** | **New Query** → **Word Frequency...**
Go to 5.

alternatively

3 Click at an empty space in area (**3**).
4 Right-click and select **New Query** → **Word Frequency...**

The **Word Frequency Query** dialog box now appears:

The **Finding matches** slider is the same as described under **Text Search Queries** (see page 185).

5   When choosing *Selected Items* from the **Of** drop-down list and then [**Select...**] the **Select Project Items** dialog box appears and is used like a Text Search Query.

6   When items and other options have been decided, then click [**Run**].

The result may look like this, with the *Summary* tab open by default:

Word	Length	Count	Weighted Percentage (%)
volunteer	9	308	1.55
work	4	287	1.44
time	4	280	1.41
what	4	255	1.28
have	4	247	1.24
about	5	238	1.20
like	4	232	1.17
volunteering	12	185	0.93
your	4	177	0.89
volunteers	10	172	0.87
people	6	170	0.86
think	5	165	0.83
some	4	129	0.65
just	4	125	0.63

Select *one* word (it is not possible to select more than one), right-click and the following options appear:

- *Open Node Preview* (or double-click or key command [**Ctrl**] + [**Shift**] + [**O**])
  Opens like any node with search words and synonyms highlighted with Narrow Coding Context (5 words).
- *Run Text Search Query*
  The **Text Search Query** dialog box appears with the search words and synonymes transferred to the search criteria. The options Selected Items is inherited from the **Word Frequency Query** dialog box. The dialog box can be edited before you run it.
- *Export List...*
- *Print List...*
- *Create As Node...*
  Creates a node with the search words and synonyms and a Narrow Coding Context (5 words). The Context Setting is retained in the Nodes folder or its subfolder during the ongoing work session.
- *Add to Stop Word List*

The *Tag Cloud* tab displays this image:

The size of the words reflects their frequency. Click on a word and a Text Search Query is created and run with results displayed as a preview.

The *Tree Map* tab displays this image:

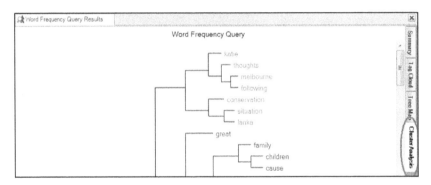

The area of each element reflects the frequency of the word. Click on a word and a Text Search Query is created and run with the results displayed as a preview.

The *Cluster Analysis* tab displays this image:

When this tab has been selected the Ribbon menu **Cluster Analysis** appears and you can choose between 2D Cluster Map, 3D Cluster Map, Horizontal Dendrogram or Vertical Dendrogram.

Compound Queries

Compound Queries make it possible to create complex queries that can combine node searches with text searches.

♦ **Follow These Steps**
   1 Go to **Explore | Queries | New Query → Compound...**
      Default folder is **Queries**.
      Go to 5.
alternatively
   1 Click [**Queries**] in area (**1**).
   2 Select the **Queries** folder in area (**2**) or its subfolder.
   3 Go to **Explore | Queries | New Query → Compound...**
      Go to 5.
alternatively

3 Click at an empty space in area **(3)**.

4 Right-click and select **New Query → Compound...**

The **Compound Query** dialog box appears. The query is divided into Subquery 1 and Subquery 2. The operator[4] between them can be chosen among several options. Observe, that the operators AND and OR are not among those options.

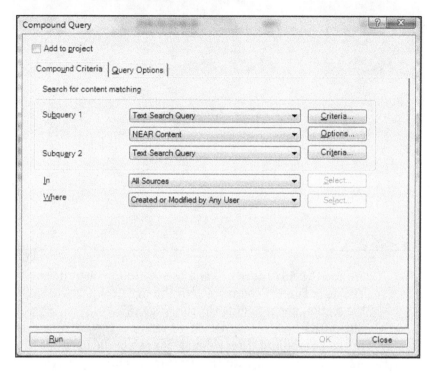

5 Choose *Coding Query* at **Subquery 1**.

6 The **[Criteria...]** button opens the **Subquery Properties** dialog box that is similar the **Coding Query** dialog box only that the option *Add To Project* and the **Query Options** tab are missing.

---

[4] See page 227 onward for explanations of the other operators on this drop-down list.

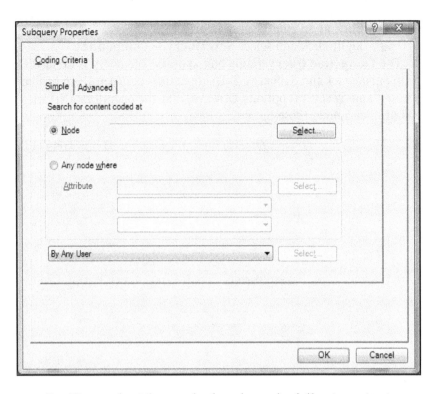

7   We use the **Advanced** tab and use the following criteria:
     The node Foreign countries AND the Age Group 20–29. See
     the section about Coding Queries, page 189.

8   Click [**OK**].

9   In the **Compound Query** dialog box select the operator
     NEAR Content and with the [**Options...**] button you select
     Overlapping.

10   Choose *Text Search Query* at **Subquery 2**.

11   The [**Criteria...**] button opens the **Subquery Properties**
     dialog box, which is similar to the **Text Search Query**
     dialog box only the option *Add To Project* and the **Query
     Options** tab missing.

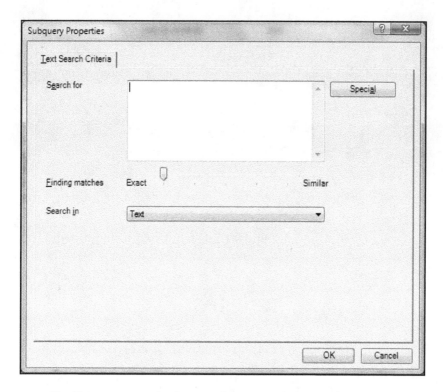

12 Type **excite** in the text box **Search for**, and pull the slider below two steps to the right which includes *Stemmed search* and synonyms.

The **Finding matches** slider is the same as described under **Text Search Queries** (see page 185).

13 Click [**OK**].

14 Click [**Run**] in the **Compound Query** dialog box.

The format of the results depends on the settings made under the **Query Options** tab (see page 221).

16. ABOUT TEAMWORK

As technology and interdisciplinarity fascilitate more and more complex qualitative studies, teamwork structures and procedures become increasingly important. NVivo allows several users to use the same project file provided that the file is opened by one user at a time. Alternatively, each member can work with his/her own project file that can be merged into a master file at a certain predefined occasion.

Teamwork can be arranged in a number of ways, for example:

- Members use the same data but each individual creates his/her nodes and codes accordingly.
- Members use different data but use a common node structure.
- Members use both same data and a common node structure.

Merging projects is described on page 51. Consider the options of the **Import Project** dialog box. If nodes with same names need to merge you select *Merge into existing item*. Remember that nodes and other items must have the same name and be located on the same level of the folder structure before they can be merged. Further, the contents of the source items must be identical.

An important concept for teamwork in NVivo is the Current User. In **File → Options** and the **Application Options** dialog box, the **General** tab identifies the the current user. When a project is open you can change the current user. However, it is not possible to leave the Name and Initial boxes empty.

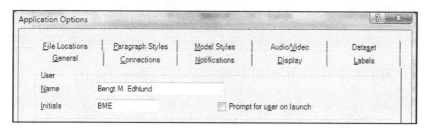

If you select the option *Prompt for user on launch* then the **Welcome to NVivo** dialog box is prompted each time NVivo is started:

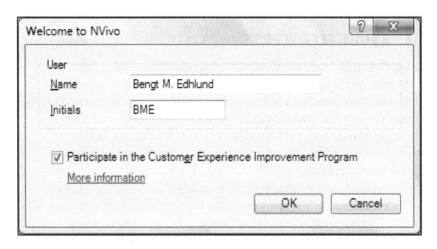

All users who have worked on the project are listed in **File → Info → Project Properties...** and the **Project Properties** dialog box, the **Users** tab:

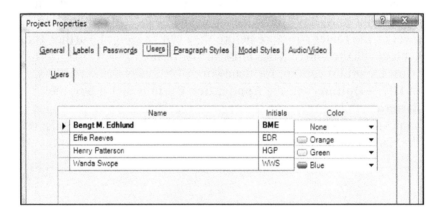

Current user is written in bold. The small triangle in the left column indicates the user who created the current project. In this box you cannot change the names but the initials. To the left in the status bar the current user is shown:

Initials are used to identify all project items created or modified by a certain user.

Viewing Coding by Users

It is possible to view the coding made by a certain member of a team.

◆ **Follow These Steps**

1 Open the node you wish to review.

2 Go to **View | Detail View | Node → Coding by Users →
 \<select>**.

3 Choose any of the options *All Users, Current User, Selected
 User..., Select Users...*

   The default setting is *All Users* and during a work session the
selected option will remain. Selecting *Select Users* will show in **bold**
the users of this node. When a certain user has been selected a filter
funnel symbol is shown in the status bar.

Viewing Coding Stripes

Coding stripes and sub-stripes can be used to display the coding that
indivudual team-members have made (see page 166).

◆ **Follow These Steps**

1 Open the source you wish ro review.

2 Go to **View | Coding | Coding Stripes → \<select>**.

3 Choose **Selected Items**.

   The **Select Project Items** dialog box appears.

   When you select **Users** the sub-stripes will show the different
nodes at which each user has coded.

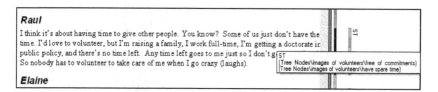

   When you instead select **Nodes** the sub-stripes will show the
different users that have coded at that node.

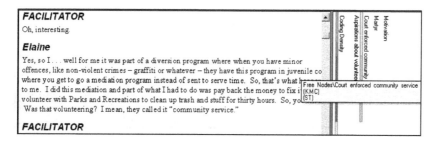

213

Coding Comparison Query

When projects are merged the identities of all users remain.
Therefore, it is possible to compare how two people or two groups of
people have coded the same material. This is possible provided that
same source material and same node structure have been used.

♦ **Follow These Steps**
   1 Go to **Explore** | **Queries** | **New Query** → **Coding
     Comparison...**
     Default folder is **Queries**.
     Go to 5.

alternatively
   1 Click [**Queries**] in area **(1)**.
   2 Select the **Queries** folder in area **(2)** or its subfolder.
   3 Go to **Explore** | **Queries** | **New Query** → **Coding
     Comparison...**
     Go to 5.

alternatively
   3 Click on any emty space in area **(3)**.
   4 Right-click and select **New Query** → **Coding Comparison...**

The **Coding Comparison Query** dialog box now appears:

5   Define User group A and B with the [**Select...**] buttons
    which give access to all users that have been working in
    the project.
6   The **At** drop-down list determines the node or nodes that
    will be compared.
7   The **Scope** drop-down list determines the source item or
    items that will be compared.
8   Select at least one of the optons *Display Kappa Coefficient*
    or *Display percentage agreement.*
9   You can save the query by checking *Add To Project.*
10 Run the query with [**Run**].
The result can look like this:

Node	Source	Source Fold	Source Size	Kappa	Agreement	A and B (%)	Not A and Not	Disagreeme	A and Not B	B and Not A
Communi	Thomas	Internals\\In	4952 chars	0,5929	89,24	9,87	79,36	10,76	0	10,76
Communi	Thomas	Internals\\In	4952 chars	0,9456	97,88	25,44	72,44	2,12	0,24	1,88
Economy	Thomas	Internals\\In	4952 chars	0,2811	91,3	2,12	89,18	8,7	4,14	4,56
Economy	Thomas	Internals\\In	4952 chars	0,9547	98,42	21,61	76,82	1,58	1,53	0,04
Natural e	Thomas	Internals\\In	4952 chars	0	91,05	0	91,05	8,95	0	8,95

Coding comparison of Wanda to Eff

The percentage agreement columns indicate the following values:
- **Agreement Column** = sum of columns **A and B** and **Not A and Not B.**
- **A and B** = the percentage of data item content coded to the selected node by both Project User Group A and Project User Group B.
- **Not A and Not B** = the percentage of data item content coded by neither Project User Group A and Project User Group B.
- Disagreement Column = sums of columns A and Not B and B and Not A.
- **A and Not B** = the percentage of data item content coded by Project User Group A and not coded by Project User Group B.
- **B and Not A** = the percentage of data item content coded by Project User Group B and not coded by Project User Group A.

From each row of the result from a Coding Comparison Query any *node* can be analyzed like this:

◆ **Follow These Steps**
1   Select a row from the list of results.
2   Go to **Home | Open | Open Node...**
    or key command [**Ctrl**] + [**Shift**] + [**O**]
    or right-click and select **Open Node...**
Any node that is opened from such list is showing the coding
stripes and sub-stripes that belong to the users who are compared.

From each row of the result from a Coding Comparison Query the *source item* can be analyzed like this:

♦ **Follow These Steps**

1 Select a row from the list of results.

2 Go to **Home | Open | Open Source...**
or right-click and select **Open Source...**
or double-click on the row.

Any source item that is opened from such a list shows the coding stripes and sub-stripes that belong to the users who are compared:

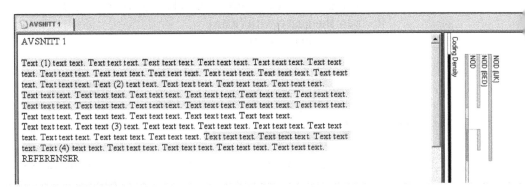

Coding stripes can always display the coding made by an individual user. This is made by pointing at a certain coding stripe, right-clicking and selecting **Show Sub-Stripes** and then selecting one or several users. Hiding sub-stripes is made using **Hide Sub-Stripes**.

Models and Reports

During project meetings for the team modelling can be illustrative and useful. Any node structure can easily be made understandable using models (see Chapter 18, Models).

Reports are created by going to **Explore | Reports | New Report**. These reports can be used to study nodes and coding made by the different team-members (see Chapter 20, Reports and Extracts).

Tips for Teamwork

- Appoint an NVivo coordinator for the research project.
- Set up protocols for file names, read-only, storage locations, backup locations, file distribution and archiving.
- Set up rules for audio and video files like file formats and file distribution. For example, should you use embedded items or external files?
- Set up a node strategy. Such a strategy can be communicated in a number of ways. It is easy to make a node template in the form of a project without source items. Each node should have 'instructions' written in the node's Description field (max 512 characters) or in the form of a linked Memo, which is easier to write, read, print and code. The node template can be distributed to team-members, saved with a new name and developed into a project in its own right. Importantly, the node template's structure must not be modified by users. When new ideas are evolved, users should instead create new nodes in addition to the node template and create Memo Links.
- Determine how Nodes and Classifications will be applied. Such nodes can be interviewees or other research items like places, professions, products, organizations, phenomenons. In some situations it is also useful to define and use Source Classifications.
- Set up rules for merging and updating the master project.
- Hold periodical project meetings for the team. Such meetings should compare and analyze data (as described in this chapter), summarize discussions, and make decisions. Distribute minutes from each meeting.

Work Procedures

Assuming that the work has come to a stage where different members have submitted contributions to the project, make sure that the team has the correct user names when they work with their respective parts.

Define a new project with a new name that clearly indicates that it is a merged project. Possibly a new set of user names will be defined for this purpose. Import one partial project at a time with **Import Project** and the option "Merge into existing item".

Items with same name and same location will be merged.

Tools for Analysis

- Use *View Coding Stripes by Selected Users* (or *View Substripes*).
- An open node can be explored with *View Coding by Users.*
- You can also use *Coding Comparison Query* whereby you compare two coders working with the same sources and nodes. This is an important option that improves a project's valididy.

Continued Work

After exploring the merged project you have two options to proceed.

- Each user continues with the original individual projects and at a certain point of time you make a complete new merger, archiving the original merger.
- Each user continues to work on the merged project and archives the original individual portions.

It seems reasonable that one continues with the first option up to a certain point and then decides to focus on the merged project.

17. COMMON QUERY FEATURES

This chapter deals with the functions and features common to several types of queries. The Filter function which is described here is an example of a common such feature. One way to benefit from the filter function is letting the filter eliminate unwanted items. For example, you can use the filter to eliminate nodes that were created later than last week.

The Filter Function

The [**Select...**]-button is available in many dialog boxes when queries are created. This button always opens the **Select Project Items** dialog box:

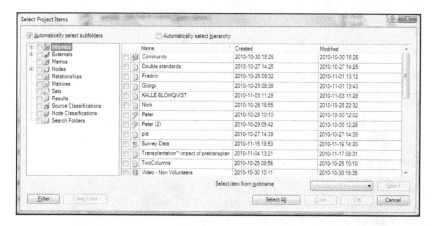

Automatically select subfolders means that when a folder is selected in the left hand window all the underlying subfolders and items will be selected. Folders which cannot have subfolders (Nodes, Sets, and Results) will select all of the items therein.

Automatically select hierarchy means that when a certain item in the right hand window has been selected all underlying items are also selected.

The [**Filter**] button is always available at the bottom left corner of the **Select Project Items** dialog box and this button opens the **Advanced Find** dialog box:

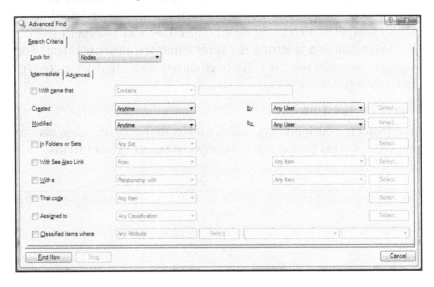

These are the same search functions described in Advanced Find (see page 174).

Saving a Query

Queries made can be saved so that they can be run again at a later stage. Let's make an example with a Text Search Query where we have already completed the Text Search Criteria.

♦ **Follow These Steps**

1   In the **Text Search Query** dialog box check *Add to project*, and a new **General** tab will appear:

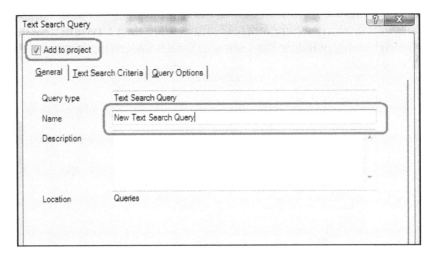

2   Type a name (compulsory) and a description (optional), then click [**Run**].

Saving a Result

The result of a query can be displayed on the screen using the option *Preview Only.* The result is shown in area (**4**) but not saved. *Preview Only* for Text Search Queries shows a list with shortcuts (see page 186). *Preview Only* for Matrix Search Queries is a matrix (see page 198). *Preview Only* for Coding Queries and Compound Queries can look like this:

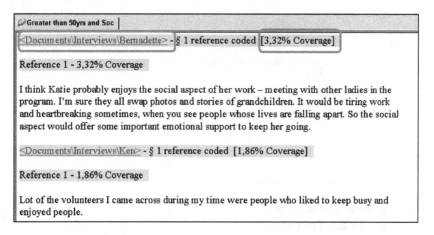

The link with the name of the coded item opens the document in area (**4**). *Coverage* means that the node or the result of the query corresponds to a certain percentage of the whole item.

The link opens the source item and the current coding is highlighted in brown. It may look like this:

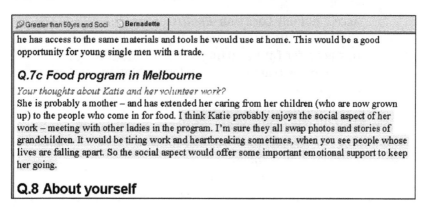

If you want to save the result as a node there are a few options to choose from, for example *Create Results as New Node.*

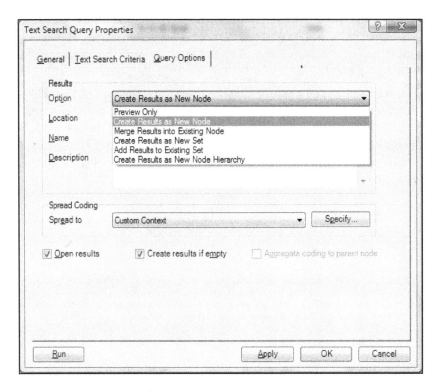

◆ **Follow These Steps**

1   In the **Text Search Query** dialog box select the **Query Options** tab.

2   Choose *Create Results as New Node* from the **Results/ Options** drop-down list. Check *Open results* when you want open the node when the query is run. Check *Create results if empty* if you want to create an 'empty' node when zero result.

3   Accept default **Location** *Results*[5] or use [**Select**] and choose another location, for example *Nodes* when you want to use this node for future coding or else future editing.

4   Type a name (compulsory) and a description (optional), then [**Run**].

The **Spread Coding** option allows you to decide other coding options. The following options are available: *None, Words, Surrounding Paragraphs, Surrounding Heading Level, Surrounding Coding Reference, Entire Source.*

- ◆ -

---

[5] Storing results in the Results folder means that the node cannot be edited.

Using **Explore | Queries | Last Run Query** the
<...> Query Properties dialog box is shown again and you may
modify or edit the query. Each time a query is run it is also saved
provided such option has been selected. When editing a query you
can for example apply *Surrounding Paragraphs* at the **Spread
Coding** drop-down list.

About the Results Folder

The Results folder is the default when a query is saved. But you can
modify **Query Properties** so that query results will be saved in any
Node location. But there are some advantages to using the Results
folder.

For example, the nodes cannot be edited when a query result is
saved as a node. As a node, query results must sometimes be verified
with command **Open Linked Query**, a possibility to modify a query.

You should eventually move your query results to be saved as
nodes in the Nodes folder. For example, commands such as **Uncode
At this Node** do not exist as long as a node is located in the Results
folder. After verifying your results node in the Results folder you
should move to a location under Nodes, where it can be used for
further coding or modifications.

When you run a Text Search Query that is saved in the Results
folder Coding Context Narrow (5 words) is activated, but the Coding
Context is reset as soon as the node is moved to a location under
Nodes. If you then should need Coding Context this feature can be
activated with a separate command (see page 165).

Editing a Query

A saved query can be run anytime:
- ◆ **Follow These Steps**
    1 Click [**Queries**] in area (**1**).
    2 Select the **Queries** folder in area (**2**) or its subfolder.
    3 Select the query in area (**3**) that you want to run.
    4 Go to **Explore | Queries | Run Query**
       or right-click and select **Run Query**...

You can always optimize a saved query so that it fulfils your
changing needs. Or you may wish to copy a query before editing.
- ◆ **Follow These Steps**
    1 Click [**Queries**] in area (**1**).
    2 Select the **Queries** folder in area (**2**) or its subfolder.
    3 Select the query in area (**3**) that you want to edit.
    4 Go to **Home | Item | Properties**
       or key command [**Ctrl**] + [**Shift**] + [**P**]
       or right-click and select **Query Properites**...

One of the following dialog boxes appears:

- **Text Search Query Properties**
- **Word Frequency Query Properties**
- **Coding Query Properties**
- **Matrix Coding Query Properties**
- **Compound Query Properties**
- **Coding Comparison Query Properties**

The **Coding Query Properties** dialog box, for example, has the same contents as the **Coding Query** dialog box. Here you can make your modifications.

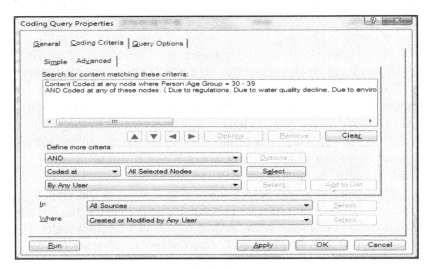

[**OK**] will carry out the modifications without running the query.

[**Apply**] will carry out the modifications without running the query again and the dialog box will remain shown so that more modifications can be made.

[**Run**] will carry through the modifications and run the query. If the option *Create Results as a New Node* under the **Query Options** tab has been selected then another node will be created in the given folder. If you choose to let the results initially be located under the **Results** folder they can be moved later on.

Deleting a Query

♦ **Follow These Steps**

1. Click [**Queries**] in area (**1**).
2. Select the **Queries** folder in area (**2**) or its subfolder.
3. Select the query or queries in area (**3**) that you want to delete.
4. Use the [**Del**] key
   or go to **Home | Editing → Delete**
   or right-click and select **Delete**.
5. Confirm with [**Yes**].

The Operators

In the **Coding Query, Matrix Coding Query and Subquery Properties** dialog boxes there are drop-down lists with various operators: AND, OR, NEAR, PRECEDING and SURROUNDING. The following charts explain the results when these operators are applied.

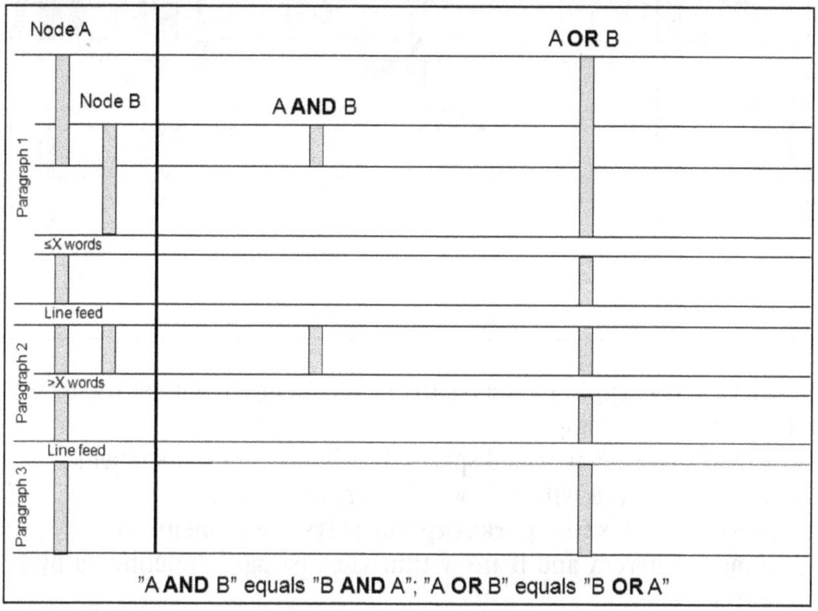

"A **AND** B" equals "B **AND** A"; "A **OR** B" equals "B **OR** A"

AND displays the elements of a document where both A and B have been coded.

OR displays the elements of a document where either A or B or both A and B have been coded.

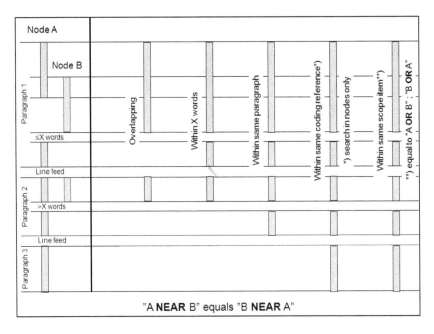

NEAR Overlapping displays the elements of a document where A and B are overlapping.

NEAR Within X words displays the elements of a document where A and B are within X words from each other.

NEAR Within same paragraph displays the elements of a document where A and B are within same paragraph delimited by line feed.

NEAR Within same coding reference displays the elements of a document where A and B are within the same node.

NEAR Within same scope item displays the elements of a document where A and B are within the same document.

Node A

Node B

Paragraph 1

Node B

≤X words

Line feed

Paragraph 2

>X words

Line feed

Paragraph 3

Overlapping | Within X words | Within same paragraph | Within same coding reference*) | *) search in nodes only | Within same scope item

"A **PRECEDING** B"

PRECEDING Overlapping displays the elements of a document where A and B overlap as long as A is coded earlier or from the same starting point as B.

PRECEDING Within X words displays the elements of a document where A and B are within X words as long as A is coded earlier or from the same starting point as B.

PRECEDING Within same paragraph displays the elements of a document where A and B are within the same paragraph delimited by line feed as long as A is coded earlier or from the same starting point as B.

PRECEDING Within same coding reference displays the elements of a document where A and B are within same node as long as A is coded earlier or from the same starting point as B.

PRECEDING Within same scope item displays the elements of a document where A and B are within same document as long as A is coded earlier or from the same starting point as B.

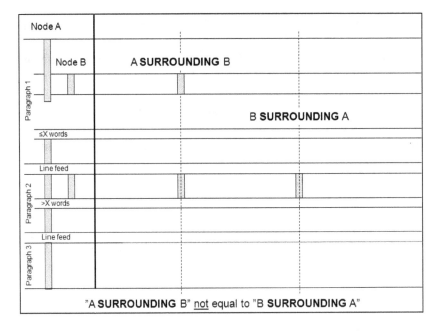

SURROUNDING displays the elements of a document where A overlaps B as long as A is coded earlier or from the same starting point as B and terminates later than or at the same point as B.

18. MODELS

Models are useful tools when a project is developing or when a project is ready to begin reporting findings. Models present ideas and theories in an easy-to-grasp way. In a research team, models are also useful during discussions or meetings.

Styles for graphical elements that should be used in future projects are created with **Application Options**, under the **Model Styles** tab (see page 32). Styles for graphical elements that should be used in the current project are created with **Project Properties**, under the **Model Styles** tab (see page 44).

Creating a New Model

♦ **Follow These Steps**

1 Go to **Explore | Models | New Model**.
Default folder is **Models**.
Go to 5.

alternatively

1 Click [**Models**] in area **(1)**.
2 Select the **Models** folder in area **(2)** or its subfolder.
3 Go to **Explore | Models | New Model**.
Go to 5.

alternatively

3 Click on an empty space in area **(3)**.
4 Right.click and select **New Model...**.

The **New Model** dialog box now appears:

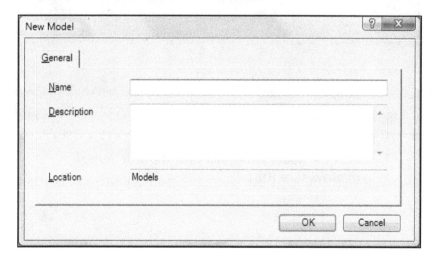

5 Type a name (compulsory) and a description (optional), then [**OK**].

A new window appears and it is a good idea to undock with **View** | **Window** | **Docked** to give you more space on the screen:

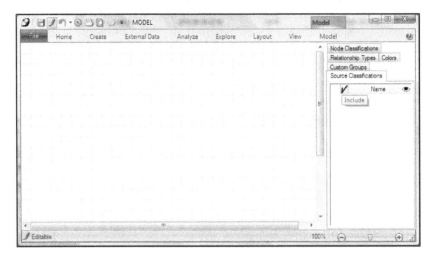

A new Ribbon menu, **Model**, has also been created.

6   Go to **Models** | **Items** | **Add Project Items** or right-click and select **Add Project Items...**

The **Select Project Items** dialog box now appears:

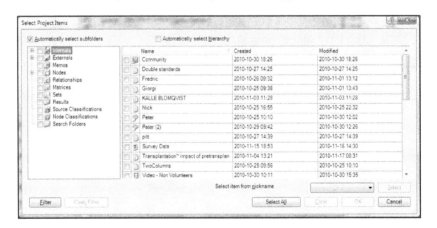

7   Select the **Nodes** folder and then the node *foreign countries*, then **[OK]**.

The **Add Associated Data** dialog box appears. The exact appearance of this dialog box depends on the type of item you have selected in the previous dialog box.

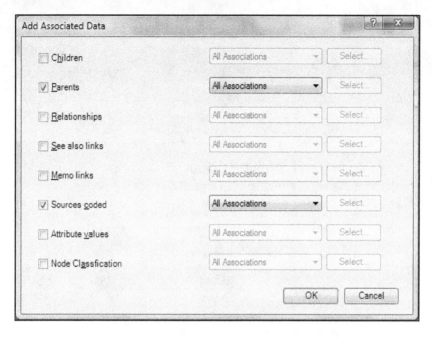

8   We select *Parents* and *Sources Coded,* then [**OK**].

The appearance of the **Add Associated Data** dialog box depends on the type of item. If you select a source item, the dialog box looks like this:

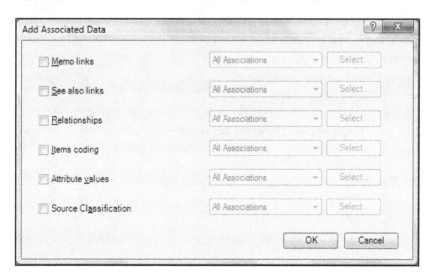

The result may look like this. There are many options to edit the image for added clarity.

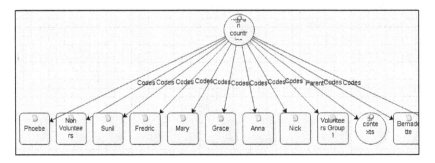

9 Go to **Model | Display | Layout**
   or right-click and select **Layout...**
The **Model Layout** dialog box now appears:

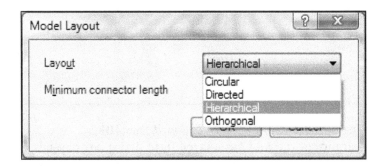

10 Select an option from the **Layout** drop-down list, confirm
    with **[OK]**.g

Creating a Static Model

A static model is a model that is independent of its linked items. A static model cannot be edited.

♦ **Follow These Steps**

1 Create or open a dynamic model.
2 Go to **Create | Items | Create As → Create As Static Model...**
   or right-click and select **Create As → Create As Static Model...**

The **New Model** dialog box now appears.

3 Type a name (compulsory) and a description (optional), then **[OK]**.

Creating Model Groups

◆ **Follow These Steps**

1 Create or open a dynamic model.

Make sure that the Custom Groups window to the right is shown. Hide and unhide is controlled with **Model | Display | Model Groups**. Click the *Custom Groups* tab in this window.

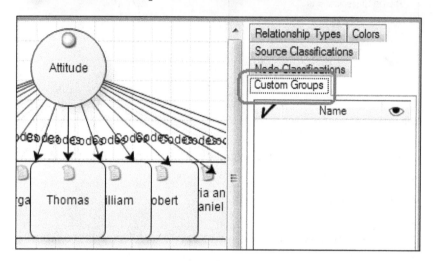

1 Go to **Models | Groups | Group → New Group...**

Click the Custom Groups tab and go to **Model → Group → New Group...**

or click on the Custom Groups window, right-click and select **New Group...**

The **Model Group Properties** dialog box now appears:

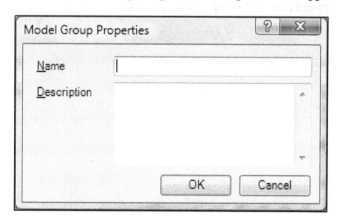

3 Type a name (compulsory) and a description (optional), then [**OK**].

4 Select the graphical items that you want to belong to the new group. Use [**Ctrl**] to select several items.

5 Check in the column marked with ✔ in the row for the new group.

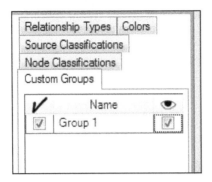

To hide/unhide a certain group, click in the column marked with an eye and in the row for the new group.

Adding More Graphical Shapes

♦ **Follow These Steps**

1 Go to **Model | Shapes → <select>** and select a shape from the list
    or position the cursor approximately where you want the shape to be placed, right-click and select **New Shape**. Select a shape from the list.

2 Select the new shape.

3 Go to **Home | Item | Properties**
    or right-click and select **Shape/Connector Properties**.

The **Shape Properties** dialog box now appears:

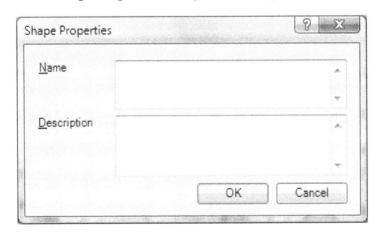

4 In the textbox **Name** type the text that shall be placed in the shape, then [**OK**].

Graphical shapes that have been inserted like this do not have the small symbol that represents a link to a project item. When such linked item is deleted a small red cross is placed on the symbol on top of the shape.

Graphical element from an inserted project item

Graphical element from an inserted project item which has been deleted

Graphical element from an inserted graphical shape

Creating Connectors between Graphical Items

♦   **Follow These Steps**
   1   Select two graphical items.
   2   Go to **Model | Connectors | <select>**
        Select one of these options:

Deleting Graphical Items

♦   **Follow These Steps**
   1   Select one or more graphical items.
   2   Use the **[Del]** key
        or go to **Home | Editing → Delete**
        or right-click and select **Delete**.

Converting Graphical Shapes

Graphical shapes can be converted to linked project items.

♦   **Follow These Steps**
   1   Select a graphical shape.
   2   Go to **Model | Items | Convert To → Convert To Existing Project Item**
        or right-click and select **Convert To → Convert To Existing Project Item**.
   3   The **Select Project Item** dialog box appears and you can choose from all existing items except those which are already used in the current model. Used items are dimmed.

4   Confirm with **[OK]**.

Linked graphical items can be converted to graphical shapes.

◆   **Follow These Steps**

1   Select one or more linked graphical items.

2   Go to **Model | Items | Convert To → Convert To Shape/Connector**
or right-click and select **Convert To → Convert To Shape/Connector**.

The graphical item retains its shape and only the link is deleted.

Editing a Graphical Item

Editing Associations

When a graphical item has been added it is possible to change or update its associations to other project items at any later occasion.

◆   **Follow These Steps**

1   Select one or more graphical items.

2   Go to **Model | Items | Add Associated Data**
or right-click and select **Add Associated Data...**

The **Add Associated Data** dialog box (extended) appears. The content of this dialog box depends on the type of item that you have selected:

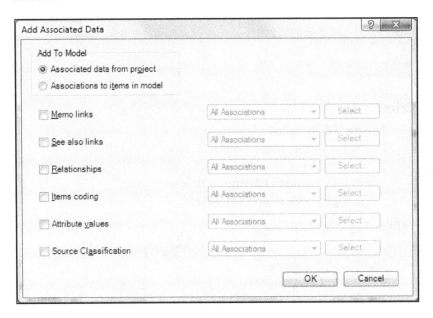

Associated data from project means that data and items from the whole project can be added.

Associations to items in model means that data and items from the current model can be added.

236

3   When the options that you want have been selected, click
    [**OK**].

Changing Text Format

♦   **Follow These Steps**
    1   Select one or more graphical items.
    2   Go to **Home | Format → <select>**.
    3   Select font, size and color.

Changing Model Style

Available templates are listed in **Project Properties,** the **Model
Styles** tab (see page 44).

♦   **Follow These Steps**
    1   Select one or more graphical items.
    2   Go to **Home | Styles → <select>**.
    3   Select a graphical template and confirm with [**OK**].

Changing Fill Color

♦   **Follow These Steps**
    1   Select one or more graphical items.
    2   Go to **Home | Format | Fill**.
    The **Fill** dialog box now appears:

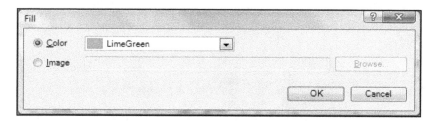

3   Select fill color from the *Color* drop-down list or find an
    image using the *Image option* and using the [**Browse...**]
    button.
4   Confirm with [**OK**].

Changing Line Color and Line Style

♦   **Follow These Steps**
    1   Select one or more graphical items.
    2   Go to **Home | Format | Line**.
    The **Line** dialog box now appears:

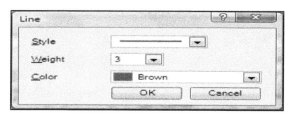

237

3   Select line style, weight, and color.
4   Confirm with [**OK**].

Deleting a Model

◆   **Follow These Steps**
1   Click [**Models**] in area **(1)**.
2   Select the **Models** folder in area **(2)** or its subfolder.
3   Select the item or items in area **(3)** that you want to delete.
4   Go to **Home | Editing | Delete**
    or use the [**Del**] key
    or right-click and select **Delete**.
5   Confirm with [**Yes**].

19. MORE ON VISUALIZATIONS

The visualizations that NVivo offers are:

- Models
- Charts
- Word Trees
- Cluster Analysis
- Tree Maps
- Graphs

Models are dealt with in Chapter 18, Models.

Charts are dealt with in Chapter 13, About Coding, section Charts.

Word Trees are dealt with in Chapter 15, About Queries, in the Text Search Queries section (see page 188).

Cluster Analysis

Cluster Analysis is a method to demonstrate graphically how related source items or nodes are based on alternative values:

♦ **Follow These Steps**

    1   Go to **Explore | Visualizations | Cluster Analysis**.

The **Cluster Analysis Wizard – Step 1** now appears:

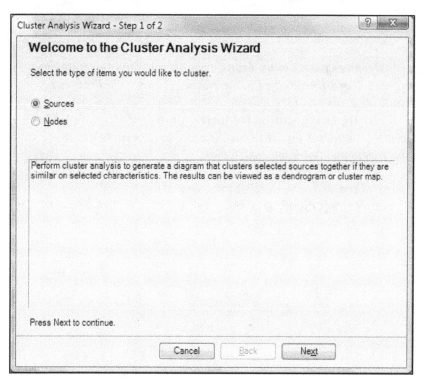

2   We want to analyze selected source items, interviews. We select the *Sources* options and click [**Next**].

The **Cluster Analysis Wizard** – **Step 2** appears:

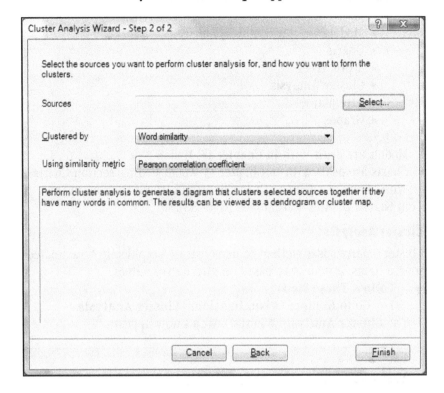

Under the **Clustered by** drop-down list you find the following options: *Word similarity, Coding similarity and Attribute value similarity*.

Under the **Using similarity metric** drop-down list you find the following options: *Jaccard's coefficient, Pearson correlation coefficient* and *Sørensen coefficient*.

3   The [**Select**] button opens the **Select Project Items** dialog box and we select all interviews.

4   Click [**Finish**].

The Ribbon menu **Cluster Analysis** appears and the first, default, image is a so called dendrogram:

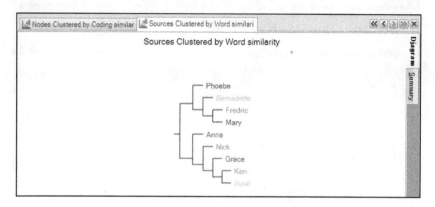

Go to **Cluster Analysis | Type | 2D Cluster Map** and the following image appears:

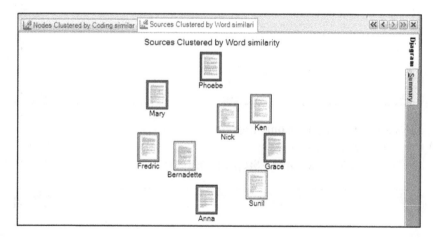

Tree Maps

Tree Maps are a way to demonstrate how a source items or nodes are related to selected information:

♦   **Follow These Steps**

1   Go to **Explore | Visualizations | Tree Maps**.

The **Tree Map Wizard - Step 1 now** appears:

We want to analyze our interviews.

  2   Click [**Next**].

The **Tree Map Wizard - Step 2** appears:

  3   Click [**Finish**].

The Ribbon menu **Tree Map** appears and the resultat may look like this:

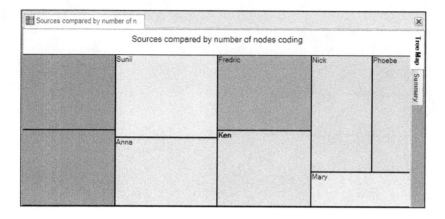

Graphs

Graphs is a quick and simple method to demonstrate how a seleted source item or node is related to other items:

♦ **Follow These Steps**

1　Select the single item in area (**3**) that you want to analyze.

2　Go to **Explore | Visualizations | Graph**.

The Ribbon menu **Graph** appears and the following image appears directly in area (**4**):

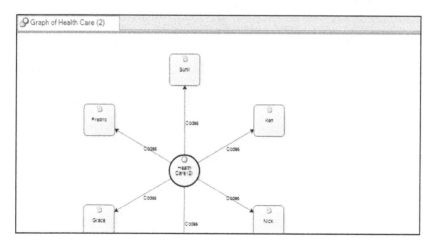

This image has the same design as Models (see Chapter 18, Models). The image can also be saved as a 'genuine' model by going to **Graph | Create | Create Model from Graph**.

20. REPORTS AND EXTRACTS

Reports

NVivo has the capacity to produce reports for certain selected items or for the entire project. There is a collection of pre-defined Reports that will appear by clicking on [**Reports**] in area (**1**) and selecting the **Reports** folder in area (**2**):

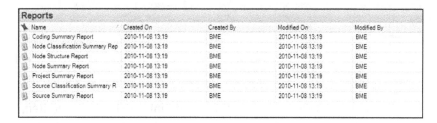

These reports can be run whenever you want to by double-clicking on one item or selecting one item and going to **Explore** | **Reports** | **Run Report** or selecting one item, right-clicking and selecting **Run Report**.

The result may be like this:

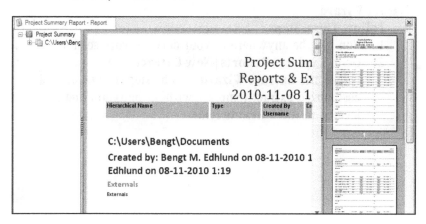

Reports can be exported in the following file formats: .DOCX, .DOC, .RTF, .TXT, Excel spreadsheets, and .PDF.

There is also an option to design customized reports using the **Report Wizard**.

♦ **Follow These Steps**

1 You may be anywhere in your current work session.

2 Go to **Explore** | **Reports** | **New Report**.

3 Follow the **Report Wizard** step by step. The result is a customized report template with an individual name located in the **Reports** folder.

Extracts

NVivo has the possibility to produce extracts from certain selected items or for the entire project. There is a collection of pre-defined Extracs that will appear by clicking on [**Reports**] in area (**1**) and selecting the **Extracts** folder in area (**2**):

Extracts				
Name	Created On	Created By	Modified On	Modified By
Coding Summary Extract	2010-11-08 13:19	BME	2010-11-08 13:19	BME
Node Classification Summary Extra	2010-11-08 13:19	BME	2010-11-08 13:19	BME
Node Structure Extract	2010-11-08 13:19	BME	2010-11-08 13:19	BME
Node Summary Extract	2010-11-08 13:19	BME	2010-11-08 13:19	BME
Project Summary Extract	2010-11-08 13:19	BME	2010-11-08 13:19	BME
Source Classification Summary Ext	2010-11-08 13:19	BME	2010-11-08 13:19	BME
Source Summary Extract	2010-11-08 13:19	BME	2010-11-08 13:19	BME

These extracts can be run anytime by double-clicking on one item or selecting one item and going to **Explore** | **Reports** | **Run Extract** or selecting one item, right-clicking and selecting **Run Extract**.

The result is a document or spreadsheet that contains names and information about the items that the Extract template has defined. Extracts do not produce data.

You can also create a customized Extract template using the **Extract Wizard**.

♦ **Follow These Steps**

1 You may be anywhere in your current work session.

2 Go to **Explore** | **Reports** | **New Extract**.

3 Follow the **Extract Wizard** step by step. The result is a customized extract template with an individual name located in the **Extracts** folder.

Exporting Project Items

All project items (except folders) can be exported in various file formats.

♦ **Follow These Steps**

1 Select the item or items that you want to export, for example two nodes.

2 Go to **External Data | Export | Export → Export Node...**
or key command **[Ctrl] + [Shift] + [E]**
or right-click and select **Export → Export Node...**

The **Export Options** dialog box now appears:

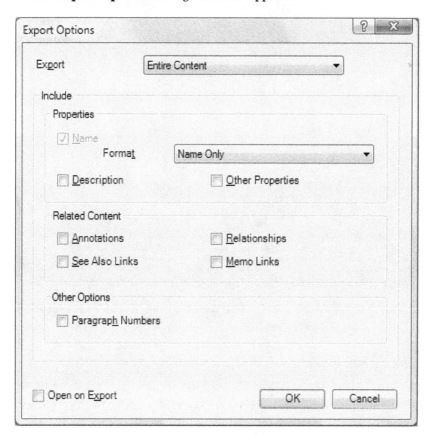

3 Select the options for the export and decide file name, file location, and file type, then **[OK]**.

21. HELP FUNCTIONS IN NVIVO

ASn integral part of NVivo is the variety of help and support functionality for users. You can choose from Online Help or Offline Help. Changes are made in the **File → Info → Project properties** dialog box:

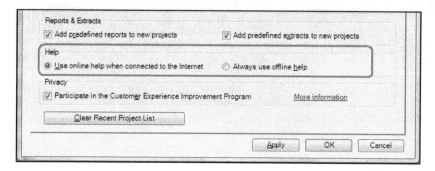

Help Documents

◆ **Follow These Steps**

1   Go to **File → Help → NVivo Help**
   or key command **[F1]**
   or use the **[?]** symbol in the upper right corner of the screen.

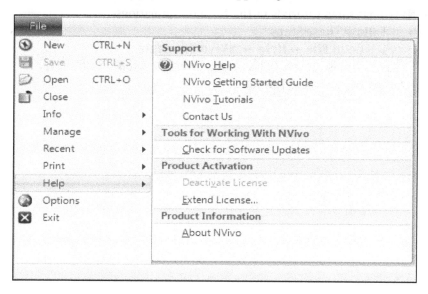

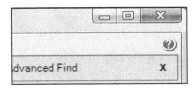

The initial view for **Oneline Help** is this:

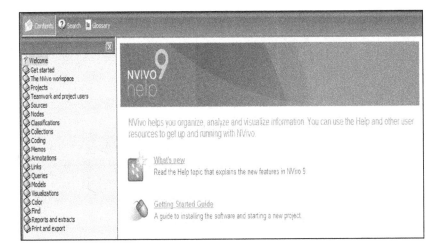

Tutorials

NVivo has some tutorials in the form of animations.

♦ **Follow These Steps**

1 Go to **File → Help → NVivo Tutorials**.

Users can also access QSR's online tutorials. Adobe Flash Player is required to play these tutorials.

Software Versions and Service Packs

You should always be aware of the software version and Service Pack that you use. A Service Pack is an additional software patch that could carry bug fixes, improvements and new features. Service Packs are free for licensees of a certain software version. Provided that you are connected to the Internet and have enabled *Check for Update every 7 Days* (see page 27) you will automatically get a message on the screen when a new Service Pack has been launched. Always use the latest available Service Pack.

♦ **Follow These Steps**

1 Go to **File → Help → About NVivo**.

The image shows the software version and installed Service Pack:

22. GLOSSARY

This is a list of the most common words, terms, and descriptions that are used in this book.

Advanced Find	Search names of project items like sources, memos or nodes. Use **Find Bar – Advanced Find.**
Aggregate	Aggregate means that a certain Node in any hierarchical level accomodates the logical sum of all its nearest Child Nodes.
Annotation	A note linked to an element of a document. Similar to a conventional footnote.
Attribute	A variable that is used to describe individual source items and nodes. Example: age group, gender, education.
Autocoding	An automatic method to code documents using names of the paragraph styles.
Boolean Operator	The conventional operators AND, OR or NOT used to create logical search expressions applying Boolean algebra.
Case	Defined as nodes with attributes in NVivo 8.
Casebook	Definition used in NVivo 8 corresponding to Classification Sheet in NVivo 9.
Classification	A collection of Attributes for Source Items or Nodes.
Cluster Analysis	Cluster analysis or clustering is the assignment of a set of observations into subsets (called *clusters*) so that observations in the same cluster are similar in some sense. Clustering is a method of unsupervised learning, and a common technique for statistical data analysis used in many fields, including machine learning, data mining, pattern recognition, image analysis, information retrieval, and bioinformatics.
Coding Stripe	Graphical representation of coding in a source document.
Coding	The work that associates a certain text element in a source document at a certain node.
Coding Queries	A method to construct a query by using combinations of nodes or attribute values.

Compound Queries	A method to construct a query by using combinations of various query types.
Coverage	The fraction of a source document that has been coded at a certain node.
Dendrogram	A tree-like plot where each step of hierarchical clustering is represented as a fusion of two branches of the tree into a single one. The branches represent clusters obtained at each step of hierarchical clustering.
Discourse Analysis	In semantics, discourses are linguistic units composed of several sentences — in other words, conversations, arguments or speeches. Discourse Analysis studies how texts can be structured and how its elements are interrelated.
Document	An item in NVivo that is usually imported from a source document.
Ethnography	The science that examines characteristics of different cultural groups.
Filter	A function that limits a selection of values or items in order to facilitate the analysis of large amounts of data.
Find Bar	A toolbar immediately above the List View.
Focus Group	A selected, limited group of people that represents a larger population.
Folder	A folder that is created by NVivo is a virtual folder but has properties and functions largely like a normal Windows folder.
Grounded Theory	Widely recognized method for qualitative studies where theories emerge from data rather than a pre-determined hypothesis.
Grouped Find	A function for finding items that have certain relations to each other.
Hyperlink	A link to an item outside the NVivo-project. The linked item can be a file or a web site.
In Vivo Coding	In Vivo coding is creating a new free node when selecting text and then using the *In Vivo* command. The node name will become the selected text (max 256 characters) but the name (and location) can be changed later.
Items	All items that constitutes a project. Items are sources, nodes, classifications, queries, results, and models.

Jaccard's Coefficient	The **Jaccard index**, also known as the **Jaccard similarity coefficient** (originally coined *coefficient de communauté* by Paul Jaccard), is a statistic used for comparing the similarity and diversity of sample sets
Kappa Coefficient	**Cohen's kappa coefficient, (K),** is a statistical measure of inter-rater agreement. It is generally thought to be a more robust measure than simple percent agreement calculation since **K** takes into account the agreement occurring by chance. Cohen's kappa coefficient measures the agreement between two raters who each classify N items into C mutually exclusive categories. If the raters are in complete agreement then **K** = 1. If there is no agreement among the raters (other than what would be expected by chance) then **K** $\leq$ 0.
Matrix Coding Query	The method to construct queries in a matrix form where contents in each cell are the result of a row and a column combined with a certain operator.
Memo Link	Only *one* Memo Link can exist from an item to a memo.
Memo	A document that could be linked from *one* document or from *one* node.
Mixed Methods	A combination of quantitative and qualitative studies.
Model	Graphical representation of project items and their relations.
Node	Often used in the context of a "container" of selected topics or themes. A node contains pointers to whole documents or selected elements of documents relevant to the specific node. Nodes can be organized hierarchically.
Pearson Correlation Coefficient	A type of correlation coefficient that represents the relationship between two variables that are measured on the same interval or ratio scale.

Phenomenology	A method which is descriptive, thoughtful, and innovative and from which you might verify your hypothesis.
Project	The collective denomination of all data and related work.
Qualitative Research	Research with data originating from observations, interviews, and dialogs that focuses on the views, experiences, values, and interpretations of participants.
Quantitative Research	Research that colletcs data through measurements and conclusions through calculations and statistics.
Ranking	The organization of results according to ascending or descending relevance.
Relationship	A node that defines a relation between two project items. A relationship is always characterized by a certain relationship type.
Relationship Type	A concept (often a descriptive verb) that defines a relationship or dependence between two project items.
Relevance	Relevance in a result of a query is a measure of success or grade of matching. Relevance may be calculated as the number of hits in selected sections of the searched item.
Research Design	A plan for the collection and study of data so that the desired information is reached with sufficient reliability and a given theory can be verified or rejected in a recognized manner.
Result	A result is the answer to a query. A result may be shown as *Preview* or saved as a *Node*.
Saving Queries	The possibility to save queries in order to re-run or to modify them.
See Also Link	A link established between two items. A See Also Link is created from a certain area or text element of an item to a selected area or the whole of another item.
Service Pack	Software updates that normally carry bug fixes, performance enhancements, and new features.

Set	A subset or "collection" of selected project items. A saved set can be displayed as a list of shortcuts to these project items.
Sørensen Coefficient	The **Sørensen index**, also known as **Sørensen's similarity coefficient**, is a statistic used for comparing the similarity of two samples. It was developed by the botanist Thorvald Sørensen and published in 1948.
Stop Words	Stop words are less significant words like conjunctions or prepositions, that may not be meaningful to your analysis. Stop words are exempted from Text Search Queries or Word Frequency Queries.
Uncoding	The work that deletes a given coding of a document at a certain node.
Validity	The validity of causal inferences within scientific studies, usually based on experiments.
Value	Value that a certain attribute can have. Similar to "Controlled Vocabulary". Example: male, female.

APPENDIX A – THE NVIVO SCREEN

The NVivo Screen

1. The Navigation Buttons
2. The Virtuel Explorer
3. The List View
4. The Detals – Opened Items

The NVivo Screen is similar to that of Microsoft Outlook. Normally you start with the Navigation Buttons (**1**) and select a certain group of folders (**2**). Clicking a folder lists its contents of documents or items (**3**). An item is opened with a double-click and is shown in area (**4**). This window can also be undocked.

For continued work you can either rightclick with the mouse (depending on its position), use Ribbon menus, or key board commands.

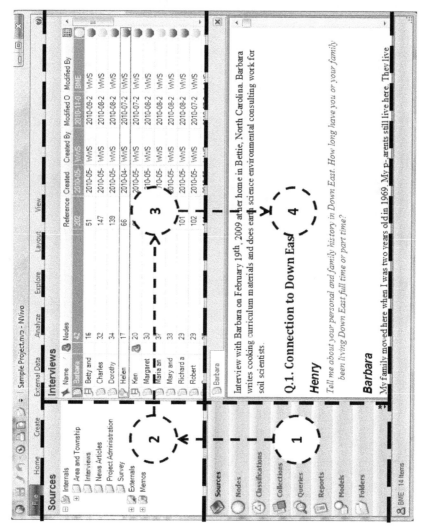

259

APPENDIX B – SYMBOLS FOR FOLDERS AND PROJECT ITEMS

This is a list of symbols used in NVivo 9. These are folder symbols used in area (2) and item symbols used in area (3), the List View.

	Internals' Folder
	Document
	Video
	Audio
	Picture
	Dataset
	Memo Link

	Externals' Folder
	External
	Memo Link

	Memos' Folder
	Memo
	Memo Link

	Nodes' Folder
	Nodes

	Relationships' Folder
	Between any two items

	Matrices' Folder
	Matrices

		Queries' Folder
		Coding Query
		Text Query
		Coding Comparison Query
		Compound Query
		Matrix Coding Query
		Word Frequency Query
		Group Query

		Results' Folder
		Result Node
		Result Matrix

		Models' Folder
		Static Model
		Dynamic Model

		Relationship Types' Folder
		Relationship Type

		Source Classifications' Folder
		Source Classification
		Attribute

		Node Classifications' Folder
		Node Classification
		Attribute

APPENDIX C – KEY COMMANDS

Listed below are some of the most useful key commands. Many of these strictly adhere to general Windows conventions. Others are specific for each program.

Windows	Word	NVivo 9	Key Command	Desription
✓	✓	✓	**[Ctrl] + [C]**	Copy
✓	✓	✓	**[Ctrl] + [X]**	Cut
✓	✓	✓	**[Ctrl] + [V]**	Paste
✓	✓	✓	**[Ctrl] + [A]**	Select All
✓	✓	✓	**[Ctrl] + [O]**	Open Project
	✓[6]	✓	**[Ctrl] + [B]**	Bold
	✓[6]	✓	**[Ctrl] + [I]**	Italic
	✓[6]	✓	**[Ctrl] + [U]**	Underline
	✓[6]		**[Ctrl] + [K]**	Insert Hyperlink
		✓	**[Ctrl] + [E]**	Switch between Edit mode and Read Only
		✓	**[Ctrl]+[Shift]+[K]**	Link to New Memo
		✓	**[Ctrl]+[Shift]+[M]**	Open Linked Memo
		✓	**[Ctrl]+[Shift]+[N]**	New Folder/Item
		✓	**[Ctrl]+[Shift]+[P]**	Folder/Item Properties
		✓	**[Ctrl]+[Shift]+[O]**	Open Item
		✓	**[Ctrl]+[Shift]+[I]**	Import Item
		✓	**[Ctrl]+[Shift]+[E]**	Export Item
		✓	**[Ctrl]+[Shift]+[F]**	Advanced Find
		✓	**[Ctrl]+[Shift]+[G]**	Grouped Find
		✓	**[Ctrl]+[Shift]+[U]**	Move Up
		✓	**[Ctrl]+[Shift]+[D]**	Move Down
		✓	**[Ctrl]+[Shift]+[L]**	Move Left
		✓	**[Ctrl]+[Shift]+[R]**	Move Right
		✓	**[Ctrl]+[Shift]+[T]**	Insert Time/Date

---

[6] Only for English version of Word.

Windows	Word	NVivo 9	Key Command	Description
	✓	✓	[Ctrl] + [G]	Go to
✓	✓	✓	[Ctrl] + [N]	New Project
✓	✓	✓	[Ctrl] + [P]	Print
✓	✓	✓	[Ctrl] + [S]	Save
		✓	[Ctrl] + [M]	Merge Into Selected Node
		✓	[Ctrl] + [1]	Go Sources
		✓	[Ctrl] + [2]	Go Nodes
		✓	[Ctrl] + [3]	Go Classifications
		✓	[Ctrl] + [4]	Go Collections
		✓	[Ctrl] + [5]	Go Queries
		✓	[Ctrl] + [6]	Go Reports
		✓	[Ctrl] + [7]	Go Models
		✓	[Ctrl] + [8]	Go Folders
✓	✓		[Ctrl] + [W]	Close Window
✓	✓		[Ctrl]+[Shift]+[W]	Close all Windows of same Type
	✓	✓	[F1]	Open Online Help
		✓	[F5]	Refresh
	✓		[F7]	Spell Check
		✓	[F7]	Play/Pause
		✓	[F8]	Stop
		✓	[F9]	Skip Back
		✓	[F10]	Skip Forward
		✓	[F11]	Start Selection
		✓	[F12]	Finish Selection
	✓	✓	[Ctrl] + [Z]	Undo
	✓		[Ctrl] + [Y]	Redo
	✓	✓	[Ctrl] + [F]	Find
	✓	✓	[Ctrl] + [H]	Replace (Detail View)
		✓	[Ctrl] + [H]	Handtool (Print Preview)
		✓	[Ctrl] + [Q]	Go to Quick Coding Bar

Windows	Word	NVivo 9	Key Command	Description
		✓	[Ctrl]+[Shift]+[F2]	Uncode Selection at Existing Nodes
		✓	[Ctrl]+[Shift]+[F3]	Uncode Selection at This Node
		✓	[Ctrl]+[Shift]+[F5]	Uncode Sources at Existing Nodes
		✓	[Ctrl]+[Shift]+[F9]	Uncode Selection at Nodes visible in Quick Coding Bar
		✓	[Ctrl] + [F2]	Code Selection at Existing Node
		✓	[Ctrl] + [F3]	Code Selection at New Node
✓		✓	[Ctrl] + [F4]	Close Current Window
		✓	[Ctrl] + [F5]	Code Sources at Existing Node
		✓	[Ctrl] + [F6]	Code Sources at New Node
		✓	[Ctrl] + [F8]	Code In Vivo
		✓	[Ctrl] + [F9]	Code Selection at Nodes visible in Quick Coding Bar
		✓	[Alt] + [F1]	Hide/Show Navigation View
		✓	[Ctrl] + [Ins]	Insert Row
		✓	[Ctrl] + [Del]	Delete Selected Items in a Model
		✓	[Ctrl]+[Shift]+[T]	Insert Date/Time
		✓	[Ctrl]+[Shift]+[Y]	Insert Symbol
	✓		[Ctrl]+[Alt]+[F]	Insert Footnote
	✓	✓	[Ctrl] + [Enter]	Insert Page break
		✓	[Ctrl] + [Enter]	Carriage Return in certain text boxes

APPENDIX D - GRAPHIC CONVENTIONS

In this book we have applied some simple graphic conventions with the intention to improve the readability and make the material easier to understand.

Example	Comment
Go to **Model** | **Shapes** | **Change Shape**	Ribbon menu **Model** och Menu group **Shapes** and Menu option **Change Shape**
Go to **File → Options**	Main menu and options with **Bold**
Right-click and select **New Query → Compound...**	Right-click with the mouse and select menu and sub-menu with **Bold**
Select the **Layout** tab	Optional tabs with **Bold**
Select *Advanced Find* from **Options** drop-down list	Variable with **Bold,** the value with *Italic;* Heading with **Bold,** options with *Italic*
Confirm with [**OK**]	Graphical buttons within brackets
Use the [**Del**] key to delete	Key is written within brackets
Type `Bibliography` in the textbox	`Courier` for text to be typed
`..[1-3]` is shown in the textbox	`Courier` for shown text
.. key command [**Ctrl**] + [**Shift**] + [**N**]	Hold the first (and second) key while touching the last

INDEX

A

Aggregate, 115, 253
Annotations, 111
Apply, 224
Attributes, 123
audio formats, 77
Autocode, 148, 158
Automatically select hierarchy, 219
Automatically select subfolders, 219

C

Classifications, 123
Classifying, 141
Cluster Analysis, 206, 239
Cluster Map, 206
Codable, 141
Code In Vivo, 265
Code sources at new cases located under, 56, 78, 105
Coding, 155, 157
Coding Comparison Queries, 214
Coding Context, 165
Coding Density Bar, 166, 167
Coding Excerpt, 162, 164
Coding Queries, 189
Coding Stripes, 166
 Sub-Stripes, 216
color marking, 18
Compound Queries, 206
Connection Map, 181
Context Words, 188
Copy, 48, 202
Copy Project, 53
Copyright, 2
Coverage, 162, 221, 254
Create descriptions, 56, 78, 105
Create Results as New Node, 221
Create results if empty, 222

creating
 a Child Node, 117
 a Classification, 124
 a Document, 57
 a folder, 46
 a Media Item, 79
 a Memo Link, 107
 a Memo Link and a Memo, 107
 a Model, 229
 a Node, 115
 a Picture Log, 96
 a Relationship, 119
 a Relationship Type, 118
 a See Also Link, 109, 110
 a Set, 47
 a Static Model, 232
 a table, 69
 an Annotation, 111
 an Attribute, 126
 an Hyperlink, 112
 Model Groups, 233
 queries, 183
 subfolders, 46
current node(s), 155
current user, 25, 211

D

Datasets, 141
deleting
 a Classification or an Attribute, 128
 a Document, 60
 a Folder, 46
 a Memo, 108
 a Memo Link, 108
 a Model, 238
 a Node, 116
 a Parent Node, 117
 a Picture Item, 101
 a Query, 224
 a Relationship, 122
 a Relationship Type, 119
 a See Also Link, 111